War or Peace: Issues That Impact Marriage

by Buddy and Susan Showalter

Dedication

To our two awesome sons, John and Joshua and
John's amazing wife Blake.
We are so thankful God blessed us with you.

Acknowledgements

We want to thank Tom and Mary Hunt for being godly
mentors and friends to us all these years. Thanks to
Dr. James Dobson and the staff of Focus on the
Family for helping shape our marriage and parenting
approach.

Contents

Dedication iii

Acknowledgements iii

Preface vii

Foreword ix

Chapter 1: Faith 1

Chapter 2: Communication and Roles 17

Chapter 3: Money 37

Chapter 4: In-laws 55

Chapter 5: Sex 63

Chapter 6: Parenting 83

Resources 109

About the Authors 110

Preface

The paradox of creating and sustaining a successful marriage is that it can be amazingly simple yet extraordinarily complicated – exceptionally rewarding but extremely challenging. There are many issues that husbands and wives will encounter together in their marital journey. In our 27 years of marriage and countless hours spent counseling young couples before they married and other couples struggling in their relationship, we have narrowed the list to the following topics that we think have the biggest potential for war or peace in marriage:

- Faith
- Communication and Roles
- Money
- In-laws
- Sex
- Parenting

We are followers of Jesus, we approach life and counseling from a Christ-centered, biblical perspective. While we are not professional counselors, the way we attempt to live, model, and advise others is based on the timeless principles of God's Word. We have found this approach to be the biggest stabilizing force in our lives and marriage. It brings peace and joy out of the chaotic world in which we live. We have also seen these principles positively impact the marriages of couples God has brought into our lives.

This book has as its origin the scriptures you will find referenced in each chapter. That was our starting point in the early days of our counseling ministry at Destiny Church. As we met with other couples and shared our stories of what God has done and continues to do in our marriage, we began writing them down. The questions at the end of each chapter are a practical way for you and your spouse, or future spouse, to discuss issues that you are either currently dealing with or will likely encounter someday in your marriage.

If you are not yet married, we hope you find these topics to be helpful as you contemplate a new chapter in your lives. In fact, we hope that many of you will explore these topics even before you get engaged. Often, once the ring is on her finger, it is very difficult to turn back. If you are already married, perhaps the advice shared here will help you get past a hurdle that is keeping you from experiencing a healthy, fulfilling, and peaceful life together.

Foreword

My name is Greg, and I am NOT a counselor! There I said it. The problem with this confession is that I am a pastor, and by definition I am supposed to be able to counsel people. I often joke that people who come to me for counseling end up having to get professional help just to get over the experience. Don't get me wrong. I really love people, and I always want to help them. I have many wonderful role models who have poured their lives into me, and that alone has imparted wisdom that I can share with others. But outside of what I call triage counseling, I do my best to send everyone I can to Buddy and Susan Showalter.

That was all working very fine for me until the day that Buddy and Susan's oldest son John and his fiancé Blake asked me to do their premarital counseling. I tried to get them to go to Buddy and Susan, but they refused…they mumbled something about that being very awkward. Because I deeply love this family, I decided to bite the bullet and actually try to be a good pastor.

So the very first thing I did was go to Buddy and ask for help. And he handed me an early draft of the book you are about to read. I didn't get past the first chapter until I pulled my wife, Pam into the mix. I would read a chapter and then hand her that section of the manuscript while I read the next chapter.

We've known Buddy and Susan for almost two decades. We've been very close friends, and our children grew up with their children. We have always held the Showalters in high regard. But after reading this book, our respect for them grew even more. They have taken the very challenging and complicated subject of marriage and broken it down by topic. Then they offer simple, yet godly and profound insights into marriage that serve couples at every level. In fact, as we read the manuscript, we forgot that we were using this material for *their* kids, and we started talking about how we could improve our own marriage using these biblical concepts.

I still try to send everyone who needs counseling to Buddy and Susan Showalter. That will probably not change. But if I ever find myself in this predicament again, I now have one of the best resources for premarital counseling ever. And that's good. Because, at this writing, Buddy and Susan have another unmarried son, Josh!

Greg Wigfield
Senior Pastor
Destiny Church

Chapter 1: Faith

One of the most important issues in marriage that can either be a tremendous blessing or an almost overwhelming area of tension is the spiritual dimension. We think the main reason our marriage thrives is that we each have a deep and abiding love for Jesus. That has been the constant in our lives – our rock.

Our Personal Stories
We want to share our personal stories with you for several reasons. One, it will help you better understand how our experiences have shaped who we are individually and as a couple. Second, we hope you see that God prepared both of us for each other. Before we even knew the other existed, God was working in us to mold us – like the proverbial Potter and clay – He knew how we would complement and complete each other. Finally, we hope you will see how faith played a key role in our decision making process.

Buddy's Testimony
I grew up on a farm in Virginia. As the oldest of three boys, I learned a work ethic from a young age and can now truly appreciate how that has impacted my life. My father modeled hard work for us. He was the middle child of a huge family – also farmers. When farming didn't quite pay all the bills, he got a second job as a rural mail carrier for the U.S. Postal Service.

He would be up before daylight and in the post office sorting mail for his route. He typically returned a little after noon and worked until dark on the farm.

My mom was a nurse, but soon after my youngest brother was born, she was able to stay at home with us full-time. She was a great cook, and I always remember meals around the table with the whole family – another great life lesson modeled for me.

I graduated from Virginia Tech with an engineering degree in 1986. Through the career center and one of my engineering professors, I ended up with a couple of job offers, but both far from home. I ended up in Madison, Wisconsin in my first job – alone in a city where I would make the most important decision of my life.

You see, I grew up going to church with my family, but did not learn what it meant to have a personal relationship with Jesus Christ until that first year in my new environment. By providence, God led me to a loving, Bible-teaching fellowship of believers called Westwood Christian Church. I remember my first Sunday, Doug Dykstra the preacher there opened the Bible, read a passage, and then began explaining what that passage meant and how I could apply it to my life. It was so different, as I had not seen that done before, and I was hooked. Thus began my spiritual journey that just a little over a year later – on September 23, 1987 – led me to accept Jesus Christ as Lord of my life and be obedient to Him in baptism.

Susan's Testimony and How We Met
In Southeast Asia where I was born – the youngest of seven – there were basically two main religions: Catholicism and Buddhism. I grew up with the latter. I remember burning incense, offering food, and praying to Buddha, but nothing made sense to me. At the temple, the adults would chant things I did not understand and did not have life application. Food and fellowship afterwards were always great, so I looked forward to that! When I was 10 years-old, my family moved here to the U.S. where I grew up in Seattle. In junior high school, I had an experience I will never forget.

At our house in West Seattle, we had a large six-foot wide window in the living room and the back of the couch was up against the lower part of that window. One early evening, in eighth grade, I was kneeling on the couch, arms folded and resting on the back pillows, looking out onto the street and beyond that into the sky as the sun was setting. As I looked at the sunset, I wondered if there was a god, much more real and powerful than the Buddha statue I grew up with – perhaps a god who was in charge of that sunset and in charge over all mankind. The thoughts stopped there without being fulfilled with an answer. Life went on as usual.

In my late teens and early 20s, I began to wonder about a lot of things. I wondered how human beings came into existence, what purpose was there to life, where do we go after we die, etc. I was imagining life from a bird's-eye view. Every day, people wake up, go

3

to work in buildings, and then, leave the buildings and go back into smaller buildings called houses. From a crow's nest, people probably looked like little ants methodically leaving the ant hills, going to other hills, and then going back to their original ant hills. I thought to myself, 'What was life's purpose?'

At that time, I had a terrific supervisory position with the City of Seattle while attending college at night. I was applying everything I learned at school to my job and was rewarded nicely at work for that. I also did runway modeling part-time with a local department store as well as with high-end boutiques, modeling 20-somethings fashion. So in others' eyes, I looked successful. However, deep down inside, I felt empty. The highs after modeling shows were met with the return of the empty feelings. The search to satisfy the question of 'What was the point of life?' relentlessly followed me. But there was no one with whom I could discuss my questions.

One day, a coworker whom I had helped with her wedding asked me to join her and her new husband on a chartered fishing trip. The event itself did not excite me but what did interest me was the fact that they wanted me to meet his son who was my age. I agreed to meet them at the dock in northwest Seattle. The date was September 23, 1988.

My friends paid for all our fishing licenses and we proceeded to board the ship. We scoped out a spot and began unpacking food while we waited for their son to arrive; he never showed. Those were the days before cell phones, so my co-worker could not call him. However, I began to notice a really good-looking guy in a green Izod pullover windbreaker, who seemed to always be looking at me every time I looked his way!

After a couple of hours on the boat, he initiated a conversation. I learned we had a lot in common but also learned that he lived in Wisconsin. This was a major disappointment as the thought of the possibility of getting asked out was probably slim since he didn't live in the area, rather two thousand miles away!

To my surprise, at the end of the four-hour fishing trip, as the boat was docking, he asked if I wanted to have dinner with him. I agreed and got the address where he was staying to pick him up since he didn't have a rental car. Although I knew Seattle well, especially the University District, I got majorly lost as the clock ticked later and later. You see, in Seattle, Interstate 5 runs north and south. All addresses west of I-5 have "W" for west, and addresses east of I-5 have "E" for east. Not knowing this, he gave me the address with NE instead of NW. So I kept looking for the address east of I-5, in the dark. Just when I was about to give up, something told me to go west of I-5. I did and found it. By then, I was 45 minutes late! But again, something told me to just stay in the car next to the curb. After sitting there a few minutes, there was a knock on the passenger side window. It was him!

We went out that night and later found ourselves at Denny's, a 24-hour restaurant, until 2:00 a.m. – well past my bed time! During our very enjoyable conversation, not only did we learn we had a lot in common, but we discussed subjects such as where mankind originated, the big bang theory (this was long before the T.V. series began), and primordial soup. I asked him for his thoughts and that was when he explained to me that mankind was created by our creator God. The conversation continued with the topic of mankind's purpose. Bingo! It was exactly what I had been needing to discuss with someone – anyone – and there had been no one until this point in time! To make a long story longer, he was able to share the whole gospel with me. He shared his testimony and the fact that it was exactly one year ago to the day that he had given his life to Christ. I was thrilled because what he shared were answers to questions that had followed me from my late teens, and linked back to the thoughts I had looking at the sunset that one evening when I was in junior high.

After our time at the restaurant, I dropped him off where he was staying and I thought I would never see him again. However, within days, Buddy wrote me a seven-page letter with scriptures referencing the things we had discussed at dinner: creation, sin, salvation in Jesus, etc. Along with that was an NIV study Bible which I still have. I began attending a non-denominational, evangelical church and we also stayed in touch by phone calls and letters. I soaked up God's Word like a sponge, attended church Sunday mornings and Sunday evenings, and participated in the singles group which, at the time, consisted of teens and those in their early 20's.

Although I couldn't pinpoint what had been missing in my life until then, it was while hanging out with Christians in the singles group that I saw the joy these people had despite circumstances. They seemed to have purpose with their existence. Both of these were intriguing to me. Even though I did not know how to say the name and number combination of verses such as Romans 3:23, or even how to find most books in the Bible, I realized they had what I longed for. Just short of two months of whole-hearted devotion to church attendance, learning about sin and its eternal consequences, Jesus's love and sacrifice, reading the Bible, and hanging out with the singles, I knew I needed and wanted Jesus in my life. On November 15, 1988, I gave my life to Him with a public confession and water baptism.

Our Courtship – Buddy's Perspective
A few weeks after Susan's baptism, I flew to Seattle to spend Thanksgiving week with her. That's when we decided to give a long-distance relationship a try. This was before the days of email and cell phones, and long-distance calls were costly. That really caused us to minimize the chit-chat and deal with important issues in our conversations.

Susan flew to Wisconsin in February for a week. It was during this trip while driving to Chicago for the day that we discussed our thoughts about kids and family life. This was pretty much the clincher for me. I think we both recognized at that point where God seemed to be leading us.

Over the next month, I continued praying about this big decision. I was a fairly new Christian, so I sought advice from godly friends and mentors. I had never fasted before, but I thought that this might be a good time to do so. I spent a day fasting and praying and asking God for confirmation about something I knew would be a life changing decision. He gave me the peace I needed and I headed to the jewelry store to purchase the ring.

In March, I again flew to Seattle – this time to surprise Susan with the ring. Her friends from church were in on it and helped facilitate the surprise visit. That evening while sitting on her friend's couch, I asked her to marry me. I still tease her because she squealed and threw her arms around me, but I don't recall her ever saying yes. She did let me put the ring on her finger, so I guess it still counts.

We originally considered being married on September 23 since that date was pretty significant over the previous 2 years, but decided we didn't want to wait that long. So, we chose July 1, 1989 and started planning.

Since we both attended churches in our respective cities, we decided to ask each of our pastors to provide premarital counseling. Many of the principles you will read in this book came from those godly pastors and their wives whom we love and trust.

The Most Important Thing

The decision to get married is a very important one and one that should not be taken lightly. However, the most important decision you will ever make in your life will impact where you spend eternity. Here is what Jesus had to say about this issue:

> **John 14:6** Jesus told him, "I am the way, the truth, and the life. No one can come to the Father except through me."

Before you make the second most important decision in your life – "whom should you marry?" – you need to evaluate the question that will impact every other area of your life, including your marriage. What will you do about Jesus? You could decide, as many do, that He is a great teacher and prophet, and just relegate Him to special occasions such as Christmas and Easter. You might even decide that attending church regularly is a good idea if you don't already do so. But sitting in church on Sunday doesn't make you a Christ follower any more than sitting in a garage makes you a car.

What we are talking about here is not "religion" but a personal relationship with the Creator of the Universe. If you have never made that decision, then we want to encourage you with every fiber of our beings to do so. It will change your life and your eternity. If you don't know how, pray to God to save you and then look for a bible teaching church in your community where you can find answers to your questions and grow spiritually with other followers of Jesus. Here is what God promises:

Hebrews 11:6 And it is impossible to please God without faith. Anyone who wants to come to him must believe that God exists and that he rewards those who sincerely seek him.

Are You on the Same Page Spiritually?

This leads us to a discussion of one of the six issues that we believe can either be a tremendous blessing or one of the biggest potential conflicts in marriage – spiritual matters. Are you both on board with the idea of creating a Christ-centered biblical marriage and family?

Here is what the Bible has to say about this idea of spiritual harmony in a relationship:

> **2 Corinthians 6:14-15** (WEB) Don't be unequally yoked with unbelievers, for what fellowship have righteousness and iniquity? Or what fellowship has light with darkness? What agreement has Christ with Belial? Or what portion has a believer with an unbeliever?

A yoke is a type of harness used to connect two large animals together to pull a plow or some other heavy load. Once "yoked" together, the two animals are pretty much stuck together. One can't go anywhere without the other. If one decides to run, the other has to run as well. If one decides to lay down, the other has to do so as well. Neither can do their own thing without causing considerable pain or discomfort to the other.

Do you see the picture being painted here? If one of you has decided as we discussed earlier to be a wholly devoted follower of Christ and the other has not, there will inevitably be conflict in your marriage. You will have to deal with questions like these:

- Do we go to church every Sunday?
- What church do we attend?
- Do we give money to the church? If so, how much?
- Do the kids have to go to church if they don't want to go?
- Will we attend home-based groups and other mid-week church events?

We have found that being equally yoked in our relationship has made a tremendous difference in our lives. We are both committed to our faith and a local church which allows us to be together as a couple and as a family regularly during the week. We are in agreement about attending church every Sunday and our two sons grew up going to church every Sunday. We made that an integral part of our lives and our routine. It was a priority over sports, and even when travelling for vacations we made it a point to check out other churches.

Unfortunately, there are many couples who aren't in agreement about the priority of faith in their lives and marriage. This leads to conflict when one spouse wants to play golf or let the kids get involved in sports that interfere with church on Sunday. It sometimes means only one spouse is praying with the children before bedtime or at meals. Even if there is no conflict, there is a sense of loneliness as one spouse does all the "spiritual stuff" while the other simply tolerates it.

That is not the way God intends it to be. He longs for a deep personal relationship with each of you and wants to bless your marriage as you grow closer to Him and each other. Which leads us to our next point of discussion.

Are you Each Growing Spiritually?

Your personal relationship with the Lord will be the biggest contributing factor to a successful marriage. One of the best visual illustrations of this is shown below. As you grow closer to God on your spiritual journey through life, you will grow closer to each other as husband and wife.

The idea here is that of priority. Your relationship with Jesus has to be numero uno. If you neglect nurturing that vital link or get the priorities out of order, your other relationships will not be as vibrant and healthy as they can be.

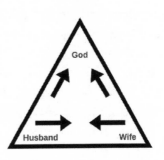

To continue to grow spiritually, you each should be daily communicating with God. We have found that a daily time of bible study and prayer is vital to maintaining and growing that relationship. Again, God longs for that fellowship and will bless you individually and as a couple as you honor and obey Him.

We believe that we are stronger spiritually as a couple than we are individually. After all, it was God's idea to create the institution of marriage.

Marriage was God's Idea from the Beginning
You will likely hear in many wedding ceremonies, the idea that marriage was God's design from the beginning of creation.

> **Genesis 2:18, 21, 22** Then the LORD God said, "It is not good for the man to be alone. I will make a helper who is just right for him." So the LORD God caused the man to fall into a deep sleep. While the man slept, the LORD God took out one of the man's ribs and closed up the opening. Then the LORD God made a woman from the rib, and he brought her to the man.

Jesus later reinforced the idea of marriage as a lifetime commitment.

> **Matthew 19:4-6** "Haven't you read the Scriptures?" Jesus replied. "They record that from the beginning 'God made them male and female.'" And he said, "'This explains why a man leaves his father and mother and is joined to his wife, and the two are united into one.' Since they are no longer two but one, let no one split apart what God has joined together."

However, the religious leaders in Jesus day were not convinced. They were accustomed to operating in accordance with man-made laws and loopholes that were added over centuries since creation.

> **Matthew 19:7** "Then why did Moses say in the law that a man could give his wife a written notice of divorce and send her away?" they asked.

Jesus' reply illuminates the creation story:

> **Matthew 19:8** "Moses permitted divorce only as a concession to your hard hearts, but it was not what God had originally intended.

God's design from the very beginning was for husbands and wives to be united as one. This "one flesh" concept goes well beyond the physical union. It means being united as one emotionally and spiritually as well. It is like no other relationship on this earth. Neither spouse will ever have this type of "oneness" with a parent or child, brother or sister. The marriage relationship is a unique, mysterious bond created by God Himself that seems to be the capstone of the creation story. It is a covenant not a contract.

We believe that if you grasp the concept that marriage is so much more than a ceremony or legal contract, it will revolutionize the way you approach your relationship. Marriage is God-ordained and intended to unite two people together as one for a lifetime.

Questions to Discuss Together

1. Where are you in your spiritual journey with God?

2. Are you and your (future) spouse on the same page spiritually? Explain.

3. Do you think it is important to go to church every Sunday? Why or why not?

4. What church do you attend now and is it the same church where your (future) spouse attends? Do you think it is important to attend church together? Why or why not?

5. Do you think it is important to give money to the church? If so, how much?

6. If (when) you have kids, do you think your children should go to church if they don't want to go? Why or why not?

7. Do you attend home-based groups or other mid-week church events? Do you think it is important to do so as a couple? Why or why not?

8. If you are a follower of Christ, are you growing spiritually in your personal relationship with Him? Why or why not?

9. What are your spiritual gifts and how are you using them to serve God?

10. Do you think marriage is God-ordained or just a man-made ceremony or legal contract? Why?

Chapter 2: Communication and Roles

A second area in marriage that can either cause conflict or provide peace and harmony is the area of communication and roles. What do we mean by this? First, we believe that God wired up men and women differently and that each has a very distinct way of thinking and communicating. Second, we believe that God created a natural order or hierarchy, if you will, in the marriage relationship. The way some people have handled these concepts can be controversial. We hope to explain how God has revealed Biblical principles on these topics to us. Let's start with communication.

Waffles and Spaghetti
We learned very early in our marriage that we approach life and marriage very uniquely. We firmly believe that God designed men and women differently, which is part of His perfect plan. There is a reason for the differences. At times, it creates tension and sometimes bewilderment, but as we have learned to be students of each other, we have come to greatly appreciate and value these differences. It is easy to think that being different is bad or often leads to disagreement, but different is neither good nor bad. It is just that — different.

In their book, *Men are Like Waffles, Women are like Spaghetti*, Bill and Pam Farrell describe it this way: women's brains are like spaghetti and men's brains are like waffles. As we have discussed this concept over the years, it has helped us better understand how we each approach issues and communicate.

In general, the way a woman thinks and processes information can be described as a bowl of spaghetti – everything is connected. One noodle is connected to or touches many other noodles at the same time. For a woman, at any point in the day, thoughts about her husband, the kids, church, job, etc. are intertwined and overlapping, just like those spaghetti noodles. Because of this, the emotions of one area can easily spill over into other areas.

In contrast, a man's brain function can be described as a waffle. There are various compartments where different issues and emotions are stored. There's the work compartment, the wife compartment, the children compartment, the church compartment, etc. Generally, in a man's mind, these are all distinct areas with their own set of thoughts and emotions. While they sometimes comingle, a man is quite able to keep them separate and, for example, the emotions of work can typically be turned off so as not to affect home life.

Susan's Perspective on **Waffles**
It baffles me to think that *men* can restrict their thoughts to one or maybe two things at a time! However, I have come to value the way Buddy helps me deal with situations that sometimes seem so intertwined in my mind. There have been several instances where we were discussing something difficult and my mind would be churning away linking

the topic at hand to other things related to it, coming up with multiple unspoken scenarios. It is usually at this point that my facial expression betrays my thoughts because he will say something like, "Honey, there is no hidden agenda here. WYSIWYG (what you see is what you get)." He reassures me that if we are discussing finances, it typically has nothing to do with our kids, my job, his job, or the dozens of other touch-points to which my brain has connected this one topic. I have to admit that I'm a bit envious at times of his ability to compartmentalize.

Buddy's Perspective on Spaghetti
While the concept of everything being so interconnected is still foreign to me, I have come to comprehend and even appreciate the way Susan's mind works. I now know that if one of our sons is struggling with something or has been disrespectful to her in some way that my "transgressions" are less likely to be overlooked. To illustrate this, Susan will sometimes approach me with a calm statement indicating that there are "two" things she would like to discuss. I know that means that I recently messed up twice. The first incident she let slide, however, the second infraction, because it is somehow connected to the first in her mind, will typically not be overlooked, and now has company. So, I jokingly ask, "Why is it always two things?"

We certainly understand that not ALL men and women function this way ALL the time. There are obviously exceptions to these general concepts. However, we have validated these principles in discussions with other couples over several decades and feel it has been helpful for us as we continue to learn to communicate with each other. We hope it is helpful to you as well, because conflict is inevitable, which is our next topic of discussion.

Conflict is Inevitable – Dealing with it Fairly
Conflict results from miscommunication. Miscommunication is a product of differing assumptions or expectations. Learning to be selfless is a lifelong process. But, because we are inherently selfish, there will always be times when we disagree. Learning to deal with conflict in a way that is fair and respectful is a difficult challenge. It takes patience and practice. However, the rewards of effective conflict resolution are many. Here's a biblical principle that has helped us over the years:

> **Ephesians 4:26-27** And "don't sin by letting anger control you." Don't let the sun go down while you are still angry, for anger gives a foothold to the devil.

Early in our marriage, we pretty much took this scripture literally. Whenever we had a disagreement, we would stay up for hours late into the night talking and crying until we worked it out. Many times the resolution was based on exhaustion rather than reconciliation.

Over the years, we have reached a point where we approach this passage a little differently. We certainly attempt to resolve issues immediately, but if we cannot, we agree to pick it up again the next day or as soon as possible. The key is verse 27 which says "anger gives a foothold to the devil." That means you agree to disagree, but you don't give your spouse the silent treatment or cold shoulder or sleep in separate rooms or use other strong-arm tactics to punish each other. That just further drives a wedge making the conversation the next day that much more difficult.

The principle here is to resolve conflict as soon as reasonably possible – when you can think clearly and talk calmly. It does not mean sweeping the issue under the rug and hoping it will just magically go away. That just allows the issue to fester for an even bigger explosion later. Sometimes taking time to think and pray about the issue helps one or both of you see where you were being selfish and admit that. There is nothing more disarming than saying to your spouse "I was wrong and I'm sorry."

It will also be helpful for you to determine how each of you tend to deal with conflict. Are you a "stuffer" or a "spewer"? In other words, do you tend to clam-up and stuff your emotions or do you quickly vent and spew your anger and frustration. Both approaches can be equally damaging or unproductive. If you tend to stuff your emotions, things can build-up and fester. You would benefit from learning to share your hurts or frustrations calmly before you blow-up. If you are quick to vent your anger, you may be prone to saying things in the heat of the moment that you will later regret. For this type of personality, learning to wait until the anger and emotion subsides can go a long way toward more peaceful conflict resolution.

We would also urge you not to use absolute terms such as "always" and "never" during arguments or heated discussions. For example, instead of saying "you always forget to ____ (fill in the blank)," try "it seems like you are forgetting pretty often these days to ____ (fill in the blank)." Talking in absolutes is likely an exaggeration and just puts the other person in defensive mode.

What if you get stuck and can't seem to resolve the issue alone? That's where godly friends and mentors can be a lifeline. Psalms 37:30 says, "The godly offer good counsel; they teach right from wrong." We've experienced several issues where we just needed to sit with people we love and trust to help us talk through it. Sometimes when we are struggling with an issue, it is very easy to think we are the only ones having that particular problem, and no one else has experienced it. You might be surprised to learn when you do talk with someone you trust, most likely they have experienced a similar struggle and are able to share how God helped them resolve it. A lot of times, just having someone that is not so emotionally engaged helps provide a little more objectivity than either of you might have at the moment. However, this approach should only happen if you both are in agreement to share the issue with another couple. We do not think it is appropriate to "air your dirty laundry" randomly with others. Confidential one-on-one counseling with a pastor or professional is a different matter, but your spouse should still be aware that you are seeking this type of advice.

Taking the D-word Out of Your Vocabulary

We mentioned earlier not using strong-arm tactics to punish each other or try to get your way. There is one grenade that we urge you to avoid lobbing at all costs and that's why this topic has its own section in this chapter. One of the best ways to bring stability and security to your marriage is to take the word "divorce" out of your vocabulary. We call it the "d-word" for just that reason.

We don't remember where we heard it or who said it, but it has been a non-negotiable principle for us that has allowed us to weather the storms that inevitably occur. We discussed in Chapter 1 what Jesus taught about divorce:

> **Matthew 19:8** "Moses permitted divorce only as a concession to your hard hearts, but it was not what God had originally intended.

We believe that God intends for marriage to be a lifelong commitment between a husband and wife. Unfortunately, our culture has made it much too easy for couples to bail-out when times get tough. While the scriptures also teach that there are circumstances, such as infidelity, where divorce is justified, we have counseled couples who have weathered even that storm and are still married today.

The point is if you commit to staying together no matter how difficult it may seem, you will have much greater incentive to resolve conflicts through compromise and forgiveness. Threats of divorce only serve to generate fear and anger. That is not the recipe for a healthy relationship which should be based on trust and unconditional love.

It is also important that you encircle yourselves with like-minded couples and role models who can encourage you along the way in this regard. First Corinthians 15:33 in part says, "bad company corrupts good character." We have read that divorce can run in packs. If you are surrounded at work, in your neighborhood, or even in your family with folks who are divorced or think that divorce is an easy solution to tough times, it will tend to influence you in negative ways. That's why we encourage you to get involved in a bible-teaching church where your odds of finding folks who will encourage you to weather the storms are much better.

We realize that there are extenuating circumstances that might require separation. We are not suggesting that anyone stay in an abusive, unsafe environment. In such circumstances, professional counseling and involvement of appropriate authorities is warranted. However, for the "normal" issues discussed in this book, eliminating the "d-word" from your vocabulary is a solid building block for a successful marriage.

Defining Roles

While this next topic could probably be in a chapter of its own, we feel that it is fundamental to how we communicate. As noted earlier, we believe that the Bible includes timeless principles that can guide every area of our lives. While the principles we are about to discuss can be controversial in our society today, we have found them to be another solid anchor for a healthy, Christ-centered marriage.

As you read these next passages of scripture together, note the unique guidance given to each gender.

> **Ephesians 5:21-33** And further, submit to one another out of reverence for Christ. For wives, this means submit to your husbands as to the Lord. For a husband is the head of his wife as Christ is the head of the church. He is the Savior of his body, the church. As the church submits to Christ, so you wives should submit to your husbands in everything. For husbands, this means love your wives, just as Christ loved the church. He gave up his life for her to make her holy and clean, washed by the cleansing of God's word. He did this to present her to himself as a glorious church without a spot or wrinkle or any other blemish. Instead, she will be holy and without fault. In the same way, husbands ought to love their wives as they love their own bodies. For a man who loves his wife actually shows love for himself. No one hates his own body but feeds and cares for it, just as Christ cares for the church. And we are

members of his body. As the Scriptures say, "A man leaves his father and mother and is joined to his wife, and the two are united into one." This is a great mystery, but it is an illustration of the way Christ and the church are one. So again I say, each man must love his wife as he loves himself, and the wife must respect her husband.

Colossians 3:18-19 Wives, submit to your husbands, as is fitting for those who belong to the Lord. Husbands, love your wives and never treat them harshly.

I Peter 3:1-7 In the same way, you wives must accept the authority of your husbands. Then, even if some refuse to obey the Good News, your godly lives will speak to them without any words. They will be won over by observing your pure and reverent lives. Don't be concerned about the outward beauty of fancy hairstyles, expensive jewelry, or beautiful clothes. You should clothe yourselves instead with the beauty that comes from within, the unfading beauty of a gentle and quiet spirit, which is so precious to God. This is how the holy women of old made themselves beautiful. They put their trust in God and accepted the authority of their husbands. For instance, Sarah obeyed her husband, Abraham, and called him her master. You are her daughters when you do what is right without fear of what your husbands might do. In the same way, you husbands must give honor to your wives. Treat your wife with understanding as you live together. She may be weaker than you are, but she is your equal partner in God's gift of new life. Treat her as you should so your prayers will not be hindered.

Notice right off the bat that Ephesians 5:21 talks about mutual submission. We might as well deal right away with the elephant in the room which is the misconception that only wives are to submit in the marriage relationship. Submission takes different forms and what follows verse 21 is an expansion on what it means for the wife to submit to her husband AND what it means for the husband to submit to his wife. A wife's submission is based on allowing her husband to lead their home spiritually just as Christ leads the church. A husband's submission is based on loving his wife just as much as Christ loves the church – a seemingly impossible goal, but one that is clearly delineated for the husband. These passages do not teach, as we have sometimes heard, that a wife is to be a doormat in the relationship with no opportunity to express an opinion or make a decision.

We heard an elder in a church we attended early in our marriage talk about how the decision-making process worked in his home. He said that when he and his wife married, they decided that as the husband, he would make all the major decisions and that his wife would make all the minor decisions. Concluding, he noted that fortunately for them, they never had to make any major decisions.

All kidding aside, it is fairly clear from the passages above that God created certain roles in marriage. Note however, that this is not the only area in life where a hierarchy exists. We are all instructed to submit to the governing authorities that God has placed in our lives (Romans 13:1). Children are instructed to honor and obey their parents (Ephesians 6:1-3). Many of us work in organizations where we have a boss or bosses. So it should not be surprising or strange that God created a natural order in marriage. But the beautiful thing about God's design is that he modelled it after Jesus' relationship with the church.

Instructions to Husbands - Buddy's Perspective
Notice the instructions to husbands to love their wives more than their very own lives. Men, if we take these instructions seriously, there will not be any controversy in the relationship about roles and submission. If I am focused on following Christ's example, that means I am to help my wife become "holy and blameless." Those are serious marching orders not to be taken lightly. This means that I need to step up to take responsibility not only for my own spiritual growth, but encouraging my wife's spiritual development as well. It means taking the lead on finding and consistently attending church. Setting the pace by serving and tithing. Leading at home by praying and reading God's Word individually and as a couple.

Men, this is probably one of the most challenging and difficult responsibilities we will have in life, but one we must accept. We cannot allow setbacks to cause us to give up. If you are not currently praying or having a devotional time with your wife, take a step. If you use the free Bible app called YouVersion, browse the plans specifically for devotions for couples. Choose a time during the day where you can both consistently spend time reading and praying together. Commit to 5 days a week - Monday to Friday. It will be awkward at first, but it will get easier.

I will be honest and say that I have struggled off and on over the years to make this a consistent part of our lives, but I don't give up. As the seasons in our lives change, I have to look for new ways to make this a priority. When the boys were in middle school and high school, we found that sharing a cup of coffee after dinner on the couch was a good time for us. Sometimes the boys would even sit in the same room with their ear buds in doing homework while we did our devotional and prayed. I'm hoping that this set an example for them for later in life. Now that the boys are grown and out of the house, we will many times do our devotional and pray together at the dinner table. I know Susan longs for this type of leadership and example in our home and she is very encouraging to me in this regard.

Note also that Colossians 3:19 instructs husbands not to be harsh and I Peter 3:7 says to be understanding and treat wives with honor. Women are typically more tender and guys, you should not think that you can talk to your wives the way you talk to your buddies at the gym. The end of verse 7 is pretty sobering where it implies that a husband's prayers can be hindered based on inappropriate treatment of his wife. Yikes!

One way that that I have learned to be considerate and respectful of my wife is to simply talk with her. It may sound very simplistic, but I have it on good authority (Susan's) that women have a greater need to verbalize than men. Dr. James Dobson notes that during a typical day, men will use about 25,000 words, whereas women will speak approximately 50,000 words[1]. During a typical weekday, Susan and I will catch each other up on our day over dinner. If I am quieter than usual, she will jokingly ask if I have used up my 25,000 words for the day. It's a gentle reminder that not only do I need to be proactive in asking about her day and what's going on in her world, but I also need to share what is going on in mine. I have learned that this simple act of connecting with her verbally, fills her emotional tank and creates a great deal of harmony in our relationship.

Instructions to Wives - Susan's Perspective
As you read earlier, I grew up to become a very independent woman in my early twenties. So, this concept of Biblical submission was initially difficult for me. Fortunately, I have several godly mentors in my life to coach me along. I sought the Lord wholeheartedly when these difficulties arose, and He was faithful to guide me.

Some of the most difficult issues Buddy and I have dealt with revolved around money. It took me a little while to understand the concept of tithing early in our

---

[1]

http://www.todayschristianwoman.com/articles/2008/september/2.34.html

marriage as I did not grow up in the church and had been a Christian less than a year by the time we were married. Then, just when I was used to the concept, we struggled over additional opportunities for "special offerings" that God presented to us. We never seemed to agree on the amount and I would typically dig in my heels until we reached a compromise. Over time, I have seen how God blessed us over and over because of our financial obedience, and I have learned to trust and submit to Buddy's leadership in this area.

One thing that my wise dear friend, mentor, and mother-figure Mary Hunt taught me is that because of the original sin of Adam and Eve in the Garden of Eden, part of God's punishment for women was to create an internal desire for us to "usurp" our husbands' authority:

> **Genesis 3:16** Then he said to the woman, "I will sharpen the pain of your pregnancy, and in pain you will give birth. And you will desire to control your husband, but he will rule over you."

What does usurp mean? You will find it means to seize and hold by force without right. Is this the position we want to take in our marriage? Let me ask you another question – is this how you operate at work? Do you usurp your supervisor's authority? It seems that we can submit to our boss's instructions (or even demands), yet, we struggle to submit at home. This may be a rhetorical question, but I will ask anyway.

Which relationship lasts a lifetime and is more important in life – work or marriage? The Scripture and questions above really help me understand the feelings I sometimes have, and God's grace has helped me to see the wisdom of His design.

Let me be clear about something. I am not suggesting that you submit to your husband if he is asking you to do something that conflicts with God's Word. If he is pressuring you to do something illegal or immoral, you have to draw the line. As we discussed in Chapter 1, your relationship with God and your obedience to Him is your first priority.

Related to this whole discussion of communication and roles, I have also learned that my husband cannot meet all my emotional needs. I need a network of other godly women in my life with whom I can talk and pray and just share life issues. The scriptures are replete with admonitions in this regard. Galatians 6:2 says to "Share each other's burdens..." and Titus 2:3-4 encourages us in part to "...teach others what is good...to love their husbands and their children, to live wisely and be pure..." I have had that modeled in my life and am now trying to model it for others. Proverbs 31 is the chapter that drives me, so to speak, as I endeavor to do what the Titus verse instructs. As I read about the woman described in this chapter, I am so encouraged to strive to be like her. I love verse 26 which states, "When she speaks, her words are wise, and she gives instructions with kindness."

Love and Respect

As noted earlier, we believe that God uniquely wires men and women and provides distinct roles for each in the marriage relationship. What we have come to understand after being at this for over 25 years is that it can be boiled down to two words to describe the innate needs of each partner – love and respect[2].

A woman longs to be loved unconditionally and feel the security of knowing that her husband is committed to their marriage relationship. If husbands seek to understand this fundamental need of their wives and nurture it by communicating daily their love for the woman with whom God has blessed them, the relationship will flourish. Simple things such as saying "I love you" several times a day, gentle touches and embraces (without sex as the end result), buying cards or flowers, and listening to her share her thoughts and feelings, all reinforce a husband's wholehearted devotion to his wife.

A man's primary need is to know that his wife respects him. If wives resolve to understand this core desire of their husbands, it can be transformative. He will not regularly hear at work or the gym, "I am proud of you!" or "Thank you for providing for your family." He needs to hear it from the helpmate that God has provided for him – the woman who completes him and helps him to be a whole man.

---

[2] There is a ministry called Love and Respect with excellent resources available at www.loveandrespect.com.

Two simple words – love and respect. Two potentially marriage-changing concepts. Are you willing to take on the challenge of implementing them in your relationship?

Questions to Discuss Together

1. How does the concept of waffles and spaghetti help you understand how your (future) spouse processes everyday issues?

2. What communication style was modeled for you growing up? Which models do you want to follow and which do you want to avoid?

3. When you get angry, do you "stuff" or "spew" your emotions? How do you think that affects your relationships?

4. Why is it important to resolve conflicts quickly rather than sweeping them under the rug?

5. Who are some godly people or couples you know and trust to help you resolve issues if you get stuck?

6. Do you think the issue of biblical submission is applicable today? Why or why not?

7. In what ways are husbands and wives to mutually submit to each other?

8.   What are your thoughts on God's instructions to husbands to be the "head of the wife as Christ is the head of the church"? What does this mean as far as practical, everyday life with your (future) spouse?

9.   What are some ways a wife can show respect for her husband?

10. What are some ways a husband can love his wife as he loves himself?

Chapter 3: Money

You may have heard that Jesus talked more about money than He did any other topic except the Kingdom of God. Why do you think this subject is so important that it requires so much attention in the Bible? Here's a clue from Matthew 6:21 where Jesus said, "Wherever your treasure is, there the desires of your heart will also be."

We believe that money is another one of those issues that can either be a huge stumbling block to a healthy marriage or a source of tremendous blessing. Entire books are written on this subject and there are many other good resources available as well. We will discuss several topics related to money that we believe are fundamental to a healthy marriage.

Tithing
The first topic is the most important in our opinion. If you get this one right, the rest are a piece of cake. Let's see what the Bible has to say about tithing or giving a tenth of our income back to God.

> **Leviticus 27:30-34** "One-tenth of the produce of the land, whether grain from the fields or fruit from the trees, belongs to the lord and must be set apart to him as holy. If you want to buy back the lord's tenth of the grain or fruit, you must pay its value, plus 20 percent. Count off every tenth animal from your herds and flocks and set them apart for the lord as holy. You may

not pick and choose between good and bad animals, and you may not substitute one for another. But if you do exchange one animal for another, then both the original animal and its substitute will be considered holy and cannot be bought back." These are the commands that the lord gave through Moses on Mount Sinai for the Israelites.

Malachi 3:10 "Bring all the tithes into the storehouse so there will be enough food in my Temple. If you do," says the LORD of Heaven's Armies, "I will open the windows of heaven for you. I will pour out a blessing so great you won't have enough room to take it in! Try it! Put me to the test!"

Matthew 23:23 "What sorrow awaits you teachers of religious law and you Pharisees. Hypocrites! For you are careful to tithe even the tiniest income from your herb gardens, but you ignore the more important aspects of the law—justice, mercy, and faith. You should tithe, yes, but do not neglect the more important things."

2 Corinthians 9:7 You must each decide in your heart how much to give. And don't give reluctantly or in response to pressure. "For God loves a person who gives cheerfully."

Tithing is not just an Old Testament concept. Notice in Matthew 23:23 that Jesus reinforced the concept of tithing, and later Paul taught that we should do so willingly and cheerfully. Not out of a sense of obligation or guilt.

So, does God need our money? Of course not. God does not need our money, but He does desire our hearts. As we read earlier in Matthew 6:21, where our treasure is determines where our heart will follow. If we are consumed with materialism, our attitudes and the way we approach life will be shaped accordingly. Materialism causes us to never be satisfied. We will always be craving the new car or new shoes or bigger house. If that is where our hearts go, then giving to God for Kingdom work is often an afterthought.

At the other extreme, if we are miserly with our finances, it causes us to live in fear that it will somehow be taken away. We won't experience the joy of generosity and blessing others and the resulting spiritual growth that God brings about in our lives. That's why we also believe that you should pay your tithe before you pay your other bills. It teaches us to be more reliant on God for the rest.

We believe that tithing to the local church where we worship and serve is a healthy, Biblical approach whether you are married or not. It stretches and strengthens our faith in God's provision for our lives. We also get to see first-hand how those finances are used to impact our community for Jesus. If you want to give additional offerings to other para-church organizations, that is great, and we do that too, but we believe the tithe should be to the church you call home.

For those who are married or considering marriage, the concept of tithing can create tension in the relationship. Early in our marriage, this was one of the subjects with which we struggled considerably. We remember one of those nights where we were committed to "not let the sun go down while we were angry." We were arguing about our budget and tithing. The accountant in our family (Susan), who did not grow up in the church and had been a Christian for less than a year at the time, was not sure how we would pay all the bills if we gave the first tenth of our income to the church. The big spender in our family (Buddy), was pretty much operating on blind faith that God would provide. Thankfully, we decided together to tithe and lo and behold, God did provide for us! Guess that is not a big surprise to many of you, but it was a growing experience for us in our marriage.

We have also learned that the saying is true, "You cannot out give God." Several years ago when both of our sons were at Liberty University, we were both working and paying on two college tuitions. We were tithing to our local church and even giving above that for a special campaign. At a certain point, Susan was out of a job for six months. We prayed and decided that we would continue our tithe and our offering to the special campaign. It was miraculous. We call it God's math. We never missed a tuition payment. God provided and revealed to us that He would pour out his blessing on us if we remained faithful to Him. It was during that time that God distinctly revealed to Susan that He was Jehovah Jireh – The Lord Who Provides. After this experience, she made stickers for the checkbook and savings book covers labeled "God's Checking" and "God's Savings" as a constant reminder that it all belongs to Him and we are just caretakers or stewards of all that He provides.

Now let's get very specific because we've been asked this question before. Do we tithe based on our gross income or our take home pay? Jesus was asked by the Pharisees at one point about paying taxes and His response was to "give to Caesar what is Caesar's and to God what is God's." We think that Jesus meant that out of your total income (remember, they didn't have income taxes taken out of their paychecks in the first century), you pay your taxes and you give to God. Another thing to think about. Everyone pays taxes based on gross income. Shouldn't God deserve at least the same baseline? So, we personally base our tithe on our gross income. However, remember, this is a heart issue. This is something you and your spouse have to agree on and be able to do cheerfully and without compulsion.

We share these personal stories hoping that you will see that this is not an easy topic. You will struggle with this issue in your marriage at some point. The key is to pray like crazy and trust that God will take care of you. Here's a promise from Matthew 6:32b-33: "...your heavenly Father already knows all your needs. Seek the Kingdom of God above all else, and live righteously, and he will give you everything you need."

Like we said at the beginning of this section, if you get this one right, the rest of the topics are a piece of cake!

Debt

This brings us to our next topic – debt. Here are some statistics according to nerdwallet.com regarding household debt in America as of December 2014:

- Average credit card debt: $15,611
- Average mortgage debt: $155,192
- Average student loan debt: $32,264
- Average new car price: $32,086 (The Motley Fool)

Credit card debt is a form of revolving debt, while mortgage, student loan, and car loan debt is called installment debt. The latter is based on a set amount borrowed and repayments typically consist of the same amount paid each month. Credit card debt can change each month depending on how much is charged on the card.

Our society is geared toward people incurring debt. It is seemingly the norm. However, here is what God's Word has to say on this subject:

> **Romans 13:8** Owe nothing to anyone – except for your obligation to love one another. If you love your neighbor, you will fulfill the requirements of God's law.

> **Proverbs 22:7** Just as the rich rule the poor, so the borrower is servant to the lender.

These passages seem to fly in the face of the world around us. As a couple, you will need to decide if you want to go with the flow of society or stand apart. Our advice is to heed God's advice as much as possible in this very important area of your marriage.

Credit Cards
First let's tackle credit card debt, which is avoidable and quite honestly can be the biggest stumbling block to healthy finances in marriage. If you are just starting out and don't yet have a credit card, carefully weigh the pros and cons before going down that road. Many credit cards offer great perks if you have the self-control to manage them properly. Airline miles or cash back are two examples of such perks. However, if you do not have enough self-discipline to keep track of your charges and pay your bill off each month, you are headed down a slippery slope. Don't go there. You are better off sticking to a cash or debit card system and avoiding the temptation and pitfalls of credit card debt.

If you already have multiple credit cards and credit card debt, we would advise you to pay off the highest interest bearing cards first and cut them up as you pay them off. Then move to a cash or debit card system for your finances. The fact that you have credit card debt indicates that you don't have enough self-control to manage them properly and you need to take drastic steps to deal with it.

Student Loans
If you haven't yet taken out student loans, consider the alternatives before making that decision. First, is

college the right decision in the first place? Not everyone is wired up for college. For some, learning a trade or opening a franchise might be the better alternative. Some might need the discipline of a military stint to help focus their lives. For others, a couple of years at a community college might be the best and most economical approach.

If you decided on the traditional four-year college approach and have student loan debt, make it a priority to get those loans paid off as quickly as possible. Before you buy a new house or a new car or begin taking extravagant vacations, make a plan and a budget to pay off the student loans.

Car Loans
According to Experian, the average monthly payment for a new car loan was $471 in the fourth quarter of 2013. That's why we suggest not buying a brand new car on credit which leads to monthly payments. That new car depreciates as much as 20% as soon as you drive it off the lot. Instead, look for good used cars at least 4 years old that have under 100,000 miles – and pay cash. You can find one for under $5,000 and if you don't have that much saved, then save up until you can afford to pay cash.

Home Mortgages
Regarding the mortgage, if you are just starting out, you'll likely have to save up for a down payment on a house. Don't get in a hurry. If you are able to afford a 15 year mortgage instead of a 30 year mortgage, that will reduce the interest you pay over the life of the loan.

If you are able to pay off the house in 15 years, then you'll have many more years to save for retirement. Better yet, if you are able to save enough to pay cash for a home, that's not impossible. It takes discipline and sacrifice, but it is possible.

However, if you are like us and didn't get good advice about mortgage debt, you may be in a 30 year mortgage. Please know that there are many opinions out there about having a mortgage versus paying it off. Research it and seek godly counsel to determine your course. There are generally two camps of thought.

Some financial advisors would say, do whatever it takes to pay off the mortgage. The argument here is that once you pay it off, you are totally debt free and you then have more freedom to save for retirement and other expenses such as college. One additional variable is how long you plan to be in the home. If you live near family and you plan to stay put, then working to pay off the mortgage and being totally debt free is the way to go. If you make one extra mortgage payment each year and apply the whole payment to the principal amount of the loan, you can cut a 30-year mortgage to about 20 or possibly 15 years.

Others say, keep the mortgage if you have a low interest rate and invest in your retirement or other high interest savings accounts what you would otherwise use to pay off the mortgage. The argument goes that you are able to earn higher interest in a stock mutual fund 401k or IRA than you are paying in mortgage interest. You also don't have money tied up in the walls of your house. Here's the catch. You have to invest in retirement or savings to make this plan work. If you keep the low interest rate mortgage, but fail to save 10-15% toward retirement, you defeat the purpose of keeping the low interest rate mortgage. This method works well if you are not sure you will be in your home for at least 10 years.

Here's our situation. We have a 30 year mortgage at a very low interest rate (<4%). We chose the latter method because we learned too late about the former. We also weren't exactly sure how long we would be in our current home due to some health issues. Again, we strongly recommend you seek counsel from a godly financial advisor or friend that you know and trust that handles finances well. If you have the opportunity to attend a Financial Peace University course developed by Dave Ramsey, we highly recommend it. As noted, we learned some of these things too late, so if you have time on your side, try to be totally debt free.

Taxes
The next topic is taxes. You've probably heard the saying, there are two sure things in life: "death and taxes." You might be surprised to learn that Jesus specifically addressed this issue:

> **Romans 13:5-7** So you must submit to them [authorities], not only to avoid punishment, but also to keep a clear conscience. Pay your taxes, too, for these same reasons. For government workers need to be paid. They are

serving God in what they do. Give to everyone what you owe them: Pay your taxes and government fees to those who collect them, and give respect and honor to those who are in authority.

That's pretty black and white, so it doesn't require much commentary from us. If you owe taxes, pay taxes. This is not an area where you should cheat and cut corners. It's not just about getting caught or audited, although that would not be pleasant. It's about doing what God asks us to do. It's about doing the right thing. Pay your taxes.

Family Provision
Another very important financial and spiritual issue is providing for the family. Typically, the brunt of this responsibility falls to the husband, but in our world today, it is not unusual or uncommon for wives to make as much or more than their husbands. Here's what Paul wrote to his disciple Timothy on this subject:

> **I Timothy 5:8** But those who won't care for their relatives, especially those in their own household, have denied the true faith. Such people are worse than unbelievers.

God wired us up to work and enjoy our jobs. Look what the writer of Ecclesiastes said about work:

> **Ecclesiastes 3:13** And people should eat and drink and enjoy the fruits of their labor, for these are gifts from God.

Ecclesiastes 3:22 So I saw that there is nothing better for people than to be happy in their work. That is our lot in life...

Now, we are not saying that we are to be consumed by our jobs and become workaholics. That's not at all healthy. But, we are saying that we should strive to find a way to provide responsibly for our families. And the Bible says you can enjoy it in the process.

Here's a word of advice regarding the lifestyle you choose. If you desire as a couple to have one of you stay home with the children when they come along, you need to establish a lifestyle from the beginning that allows you to live on one salary. We were blessed that Buddy had a job that allowed Susan to be home with our two boys when they were young. But, we deliberately made lifestyle decisions that didn't require her additional income to survive. That takes planning and communication, but it is certainly possible, even in today's world.

Budgeting
If you truly want to become "one flesh" as a couple, establish a budget together and stick with it. Here's what the writer of Proverbs had to say about this subject:

Proverbs 27:23 Know the state of your flocks, and put your heart into caring for your herds...

Not many of us have flocks and herds these days, so we have to extrapolate the metaphor to our 21st century lives. Knowing the state of your flocks is comparable to knowing how much you have in checking and savings. Speaking of which, you need to establish joint checking and savings accounts. As we mentioned earlier, the "one flesh" concept should apply to every area of life in a healthy, peaceful marriage. That translates to one bank account. Not my money and your money, but our money.

Here's a rule of thumb for your budget – 10-10-80. That means give 10%, save 10%, and live on 80%.

As we mentioned earlier in this chapter, if you give your first 10% to God, you are saying to Him, I trust you for the rest. We can attest to the blessings, spiritual growth, and miracles we have seen God do because we practiced this principle. Saving 10% is just a good practice and allows you to have an emergency fund, college money for the kids, and a nest egg for retirement. Your emergency fund should be anywhere from three to six months of living expenses. If one of you loses a job, it may take that long to find a new one. Most states have 529 college saving plans. By setting aside part of your savings in a 529 plan, your money can earn decent interest until your children go off to school. Most are transferable as long as they are used for higher education. If you have a 401k or other retirement fund at work, contribute at least the minimum that they require to provide their maximum matching contribution. For example, many companies will match three to four percent if you contribute at least five percent. That's basically free money they are providing on top of your salary. It would be foolish to pass that up.

Living on 80% may seem difficult, but it's really not if you set your mind to it. If you limit your housing costs to 25% of your net income, you still have over half of your income for gas, food, clothing, and keeping the lights on. There are many good budgeting tools available online to help you with the process. The key is to communicate with your spouse and not let money be a battleground in your marriage.

Inheritance
We hope you are sensing through this discussion that with prayer, planning, and communication, money can be a peaceful topic in your relationship instead of a stressful one. If you and your spouse commit to living out these godly principles in your marriage, you can be a blessing not only to your children, but your grandchildren as well. While we're not at the point in our lives where we have grandchildren, we still look forward to living out this proverb:

> **Proverbs 13:22** Good people leave an inheritance to their grandchildren...

What a great goal! It is obviously attainable. You might be thinking you will never get there, but we believe it is possible and we are making decisions in our lives that we pray will make it a reality someday.

Contentment

The final topic in this chapter is contentment. Watching any football game, especially the Super Bowl, confirms that advertisers want you to be discontent. Whether it's a new car, new shoes, or new smart phone, you are urged to move on to the next style or latest upgrade. However, "next" and "latest" cost money. Now we aren't saying that you have to wear burlap and drive a Yugo. What we are saying is that lack of contentment can lead you down a path that becomes steeper and more difficult to reverse. Here's what the New Testament reveals on this topic:

> **Hebrews 13:5** Don't love money; be satisfied with what you have. For God has said, "I will never fail you. I will never abandon you."

Also look at what one of the writers of Proverbs had to say about poverty and riches:

> **Proverbs 30:7-9** O God, I beg two favors from you; let me have them before I die. First, help me never to tell a lie. Second, give me neither poverty nor riches! Give me just enough to satisfy my needs. For if I grow rich, I may deny you and say, "Who is the lord?" And if I am too poor, I may steal and thus insult God's holy name.

A closing thought for you on the subject of money is this:

Matthew 6:31-33 "So don't worry about these things, saying, 'What will we eat? What will we drink? What will we wear?' These things dominate the thoughts of unbelievers, but your heavenly Father already knows all your needs. Seek the Kingdom of God above all else, and live righteously, and he will give you everything you need.

That's a promise you can believe.

Questions to Discuss Together

1. Do you believe tithing (giving ten percent to God) is an Old Testament concept only? If you answered yes, then what is the right percentage in these New Testament days?

2. What is your opinion about credit card debt? Do you have self-control issues when it comes to credit cards? If so explain.

3. What is your opinion about buying new versus used cars? Do you have car payments? Do you think paying cash for a car is realistic?

4. Do you have student loans? If so, how much, and do you have a plan for paying them off?

5. Are you interested in owning your own home someday? If so, discuss your opinion regarding a 15 year or 30 year mortgage. Is paying cash for a home realistic in today's world? Why or why not?

6. Do you prepare your own taxes or have someone else do that for you? Have you ever under-reported income or over-reported

deductions to get a bigger tax return? Why or why not?

7. Do you think it is necessary for both (future) spouses to provide income for the family? Does your answer change when kids come along?

8. Do you think married couples should have separate or joint checking and savings accounts? Explain.

9. Explain your approach to budgeting and saving. Do you have a budget and stick to it to handle your finances? Do you have savings set aside for emergencies? Do you contribute to a 401k? Explain your approach to budgeting and saving.

10. Would you describe yourself as content? Why or why not?

Chapter 4: In-laws

You may have heard this one: What's the difference between outlaws and in-laws? Outlaws are wanted! It seems like the subject of "in-laws" is the butt of many jokes. While it can be a battle ground for many couples, it doesn't have to be that way. Let's look again at a passage in Matthew for some wisdom:

> **Matthew 19:4-6** "Haven't you read the Scriptures?" Jesus replied. "They record that from the beginning 'God made them male and female.'" And he said, "'This explains why a man leaves his father and mother and is joined to his wife, and the two are united into one.' Since they are no longer two but one, let no one split apart what God has joined together."

Leave and Cleave
The King James Version of the Bible translates verse 5 as "a man will **leave** his father and mother and **cleave** to his wife." The idea of leaving and cleaving means to change priorities. You may have grown up being dependent and closely connected to your parents. That is actually a good thing and we do not want to downplay or minimize that connection. However, when you marry, your priority has to change. Your spouse now becomes your priority.

Let's say you were daddy's little girl. You grew up feeling loved and protected by your dad - in a way only a father can provide. He may have taken you on father/daughter dates and taught you to drive. He interrogated all your boyfriends and did his best to embarrass you in front of them. But then one day (or one day soon) he walked you down the aisle and "gave you away" to another man. This new man is now your protector and first love. It doesn't mean you love your daddy any less, but it does mean that the first person you talk to about your car problem or your work issues is your husband. If you go "running to daddy" every time there is a tough situation or problem, you alienate the husband that God gave you and with whom you are to become "one."

Men, you might similarly have a close relationship with your mother. You call her and remember to send her Mother's Day cards and birthday cards. She advised you when you were a teenager about what girls like and how to pick the right kind of flowers for prom. If you are not yet married, you probably love her cooking because it's all you've ever known. Now God has blessed you with a new wife or fiancé who is or must become your number one earthly priority. It doesn't mean you love your mother any less. It doesn't mean you don't still send the cards and make the calls. It does mean, however, that your go-to gal is the woman with whom God has blessed you in your marriage.

Buddy's Leave and Cleave Story
Soon after we were married, my mom and dad invited us to the Showalter family reunion. My dad had 13 brothers and sisters, so his side of the family was huge and it wasn't unusual to have over 300 people at these family reunions. Our oldest son John was probably

only a year or two old when we went. Most of Dad's family were Old-order Mennonites. Many drove a horse and buggy and they dressed very conservatively. Men wore button up shirts and women all wore dresses. They also are all very Caucasian. Not surprisingly, my beautiful Vietnamese wife and Amerasian son stood out in the crowd.

My mom had coached Susan about what to expect and being an oblivious husband, I thought everything had gone rather swimmingly. I don't remember much about our discussion immediately following the reunion, but the following year we were invited again. This time, Susan said she did not want to go. She said that she felt uncomfortable the previous year and she didn't want to subject herself to the scrutiny again. I couldn't believe it. I was angry and we fought. But, I was unable to convince her to change her mind. So, I decided to seek godly counsel.

I went to visit my friend and Pastor at the time, Tom Hunt. I was sure Tom would give me the ammunition I needed to make my case and convince Susan that we needed to go to the family reunion. I was looking for something on "submission" or "ruling with an iron fist." I was sure the latter had to be a proverb somewhere. Instead, Tom guided me to Matthew 19:4-6. He said, "Buddy, your wife is now your priority, not your Dad's family. You need to stay home with your wife." I was stunned. That was not at all the counsel I expected from my friend and mentor. But, he was right. It was a valuable lesson that I learned about leaving and cleaving. One I've never forgotten.

Honor Your Father and Mother
We are not saying that you cut off ties with your parents or in-laws. On the contrary, Jesus was very clear about how to treat parents:

> **Matthew 19:16-19** Someone came to Jesus with this question: "Teacher, what good deed must I do to have eternal life?"
> "Why ask me about what is good?" Jesus replied. "There is only One who is good. But to answer your question—if you want to receive eternal life, keep the commandments."
> "Which ones?" the man asked.
> And Jesus replied: "'You must not murder. You must not commit adultery. You must not steal. You must not testify falsely. **Honor your father and mother**. Love your neighbor as yourself.'"

Honoring your father and mother requires balance and clear communication. There will be times when you have to negotiate where you spend your holidays. Perhaps Thanksgiving with one side of the family and Christmas with the other. You'll need to begin thinking about starting your own family traditions as well. In the process, be respectful and do your best to honor your parents. Remember, this is a new adjustment for them too. They have a new son or daughter they are learning to love.

When your kids come along, you will want to encourage time for your children with their grandparents. When our boys were young, they used to love visiting Grandma and Grandpa on the farm or at the lake. Some of their fondest memories are fishing with Grandpa or going for rides in the wagon behind the tractor. Camping out in the living room in front of the fireplace and going to Red Lobster with Grandma are things they still talk about today.

Of course, you may have to set some boundaries as well. We remember some difficult discussions with Buddy's dad about some of the television shows he would be watching when his young grandsons were around. We had established some ground rules in our own family about what was appropriate for our boys and what wasn't. We communicated that very honestly but with respect to Buddy's mom and dad and feel they honored our request.

Blended Families
Do you realize that many of the Old Testament families were blended families? Take for example Jacob. If you read Genesis chapters 29 and 30, you'll see that Jacob eventually had four wives: Leah, Rachel, Bilhah, and Zilpah. With these four wives, Jacob had 12 sons and a daughter. Talk about a blended family - and a very dysfunctional family at that.

Today, due primarily to the divorce rate, step-fathers, step-mothers, step-brothers, and step-sisters are likely a part of at least half of all families. This creates a whole new dynamic that many couples have to deal with on a daily basis. Instead of two sets of in-laws, there are as many as four. Depending on how amiably the divorce transpired, there could be additional tension with in-laws because of the circumstances surrounding the split.

One sad repercussion is that kids tend to suffer considerably in these types of situations. However, with respect to in-laws and grandchildren, if your children had a healthy relationship with their biological grandparents prior to the divorce, don't penalize either party by keeping them apart. Children should be able to build good memories with grandparents, so be mature enough to allow them that opportunity.

Questions to Discuss Together

1. Would you say you are closer to your mother or father? Explain.

2. Has your relationship with one or both of your parents created conflict with your (future) spouse? If so, how?

3. How do you decide where to spend holidays? Does that ever create conflict? Explain.

4. Have you ever had to establish "boundaries" with your parents or (future) in-laws? What was the issue and how did that discussion go?

5. What are some ways you can honor your parents or (future) in-laws?

6. Are you from a blended family? If so, what are your relationships like with your step-family members?

7. How will you nurture the relationship with your children and their grandparents? Are there any unhealthy issues with your parents or (future) in-laws from which you will need to shield your children (at least early on)?

Chapter 5: Sex

OK guys, if you turned to this chapter first, we are not surprised. But you are busted! Ha!

All kidding aside, sex is a topic that has the potential to create considerable tension and stress in marriage. Often, sex can be a sensitive topic because some people have experienced hurt or disappointment in this area. However, we believe it was created by God to be a fun, intimate, beautiful experience between a husband and wife that is like glue in the relationship. Let's look again at a passage in Matthew to which we have turned several times, in this case focusing on yet another area of emphasis:

> **Matthew 19:4-6** "Haven't you read the Scriptures?" Jesus replied. "They record that from the beginning 'God made them male and female.'" And he said, "'This explains why a man leaves his father and mother and is joined to his wife, and **the two are united into one**.' Since **they are no longer two but one**, let no one split apart what God has joined together."

The emphasis this time is on the concept of "one flesh." As we noted in Chapter 1 on faith, the idea of "one flesh" encompasses a physical, spiritual, and emotional tie like no other. When a husband and wife consummate their marriage, there is not only a physical and emotional bond, but they are fulfilling a God-ordained spiritual union. God doesn't make mistakes and sex is not an afterthought in the creation story.

Neither is sex a dirty or lowly act intended only for procreation. If this is your outlook, spend some time reading the Song of Solomon and sense the passion of young lovers. While some of the metaphors used may seem a little strange to us today, it is obvious that they were flirting and engaging in amorous behavior, yet they were not ashamed.

Unfortunately, our society today has turned sex into something it was never intended to be. In our instant gratification world, it has become almost a recreational activity. We say almost because as much as some might try to diminish the emotional connection, it is almost impossible to do so. Sex is an intimate connection and emotions run deep, especially for women.

This topic can be extremely sensitive for some women. One study revealed that one in three girls are sexually abused before the age of eighteen.[3] If you have experienced this, we acknowledge your hurt. You are not alone and it was not your fault. We strongly encourage you to seek professional counseling as this issue will affect your intimacy with your husband.

---

[3] National Center for Victims of Crime (2000).

Sex Before Marriage

A topic we deal with all too often in pre-marital counseling today is the topic of sex before marriage. To be succinct, we say do not do it! That may sound old-fashioned or prudish, but we draw this conclusion from several passages of scripture:

I Thessalonians 4:3 God's will is for you to be holy, so stay away from all sexual sin.

The original Greek term translated "sexual sin" in this passage is "porneia" from which the English word pornography is derived. Here's how other biblical translations interpret this term:

- King James Version "fornication"
- Revised Standard Version "unchastity"
- The Message Version "promiscuity"
- New International Version "sexual immorality"
- The Webster Bible "lewdness"

Some argue that this, and other similar passages, does not prohibit premarital sex. However, a Google search of the term "fornication" yields the following:

One major academic theological work that equates porneia with premarital sex is Kittel and Friedrich's *Theological Dictionary of the New Testament* from 1977. In defining porneia as fornication, it states that "The NT is characterized by an unconditional repudiation of all extra-marital and unnatural intercourse." Likewise, Friberg's *Analytical Lexicon to the Greek New Testament* defines porneia as being "generally, every kind of extra-marital, unlawful or unnatural sexual intercourse." Wikipedia

This makes it clear that sex outside of marriage is not what God intends. To suggest otherwise is simply an attempt to rationalize unbiblical behavior.

Further, looking again at Matthew 19:4-6, there is a natural progression of leaving one's parents, being united to a wife, and becoming one flesh. The order is leaving, cleaving, and then sex. Changing the sequence flies in the face of the Creator's original plan.

If you want to experience God's blessing in your life and marriage, it is important to deal with blatant, willful sin. Now, you may be saying that this sin is no different from any other sin. However, see what the New Testament has to say in this regard:

> **1 Corinthians 6:18** Run from sexual sin! No other sin so clearly affects the body as this one does. For sexual immorality is a sin against your own body.

Notice the specific distinction regarding sexual sin when Paul says "No other sin so clearly affects the body as this one does." The Bible clearly places an emphasis here on the risk of sexual sin.

Buddy's Advice to Men

Men, beyond the clear scriptural mandate, there's a spiritual leadership issue here that you have to consider. If before marriage you are not spiritually mature enough to maintain self-control (one of the fruits of the Spirit), what kind of example of spiritual headship are you providing for your future wife? If you are willing to compromise in this area, what other compromises are you or will you be prone to make? You may be saying to yourself that "it takes two to tango," but you have the God-ordained responsibility to set and maintain the right course for your marriage – and it starts with sexual purity. While it may not currently be apparent, she has likely lost a certain amount of respect for you if you have conceded here.

However, it is not too late to do something about it. You can redeem the situation by stepping up and leading in this area. If you are having sex, stop, repent, and commit to each other to abstain until your wedding night. If you are living together, make arrangements for one of you to live elsewhere until after you are married. If finances are an issue, there are ways to take care of this. You can move in with a relative or a friend. If you worship regularly at a local church, there's bound to be a family or two that would gladly accommodate you if your desire is to be obedient. Don't make excuses about budget or inconvenience. The old saying, "Where there's a will, there's a way" is still true. Just do the right thing. Men, step up and lead!

Susan's Advice to Women

Ladies, prior to marriage, you do not have to prove your love to your guy with sex. It seems that the pressure to do this is enormous. You likely have very few friends these days encouraging you to abstain from sex prior to marriage. From talking with a lot of people over the years, as well as from reading Christian resources on marriage, having sex with a man prior to getting married results in significant emotional baggage that carries into your marriage. In addition to the false sense of security, you are probably feeling a lot of guilt. It does not have to be this way.

If you are already having sex with your fiancé, you may think it is too late to do anything about it. This is not true. You can change the situation you are in and start fresh. First, repent and seek forgiveness from God. Then, talk to your fiancé about your decision. He should fully understand and accept your position. It will be difficult since you have already experienced the intimacy that comes with sex. However, I fully believe you will experience freedom from guilt and experience blessings from God. Both of you will appreciate this throughout your marriage. You will not regret this decision. On the other hand, if the man you are considering marrying gets upset or tries to talk you out of your decision to honor God, this should be a red flag. I would strongly advise you to seek advice from a godly woman whom you know to be wise and trustworthy.

Here's another thing to think about before making the decision to have premarital sex. You have the rest of your marriage to be intimate with your husband. Why bring baggage into the marriage by having sex before the wedding night? Why create the guilt? Why risk the disrespect, even after you are married? Some health and exercise literature suggests that many people still enjoy sex into their 60's and even 70's for some. If on average people get married at age 25 or 30, you'll still be enjoying physical intimacy for at least 30 years. Thirty years! And you don't want to wait six or ten months before the wedding night? Be wise. Think this through. You will not regret this decision.

Keeping the Marriage Bed Pure
Whether you are married, engaged, or considering marriage, many choices and decisions you make can affect your married sex life. That's why the writer of Hebrews gave the following admonition:

> **Hebrews 13:4** Marriage should be honored by all, and the marriage bed kept pure, for God will judge the adulterer and all the sexually immoral (NIV).

Keeping the marriage bed pure means not only guarding against the physical act of adultery, but also protecting your mind and heart from anything that creates fantasies or lustful thoughts of anyone other than your spouse. This is important because of Jesus' admonition:

Matthew 5:27-28 "You have heard the commandment that says, 'You must not commit adultery.' But I say, anyone who even looks at a woman with lust has already committed adultery with her in his heart."

Pornography and romance novels are two examples of activities that can lead to defiling the marriage bed. With the prevalence of pornography on the internet and what might be called "soft-porn" in movies and television, it is increasingly more difficult, for men especially, to resist these temptations. Men in particular need more accountability in this area. If you are not already in an accountability relationship with other men regarding this issue, we would encourage you to seek out godly men you know and trust to help you deal honestly with it.

While women might tend to struggle less with lust, romance novels or movies (especially chick-flicks) can create fantasy worlds where emotional infidelity can occur. If you find yourself fantasizing about being with a man other than your husband, that's a sign of trouble.

Another slippery slope is maintaining close friendships with members of the opposite sex after marriage. Whether those former relationships were sexual or not, it is important to establish clear boundaries after marriage. Being alone together with those former friends is unwise.

Prior to our marriage, Buddy had a female friend who attended the same church he did. There was nothing romantic about their relationship in his mind, but he would sometimes assist with simple car maintenance issues like changing her oil. He also attended events with her occasionally at the middle school where she taught. After our marriage, she continued to call him to assist with her car and even asked him to go to counseling with her to help her process some relational issues. Susan was wise enough to understand what was going on and intercepted the calls and requests. Susan gently but firmly indicated that she would accompany Buddy to any counseling sessions and car maintenance appointments. Needless to say, the requests dwindled away.

It is absolutely critical that you build guardrails into your lives to prevent even the appearance of impropriety. An example is how you interact with people of the opposite sex at work, church, school, or your neighborhood. You would be wise not to allow situations where someone of the opposite gender is confiding with you about deeply personal or intimate issues. That's a recipe for disaster. If you think this person could benefit from your experience or wisdom, then they would most certainly gain even more benefit from the combined wisdom of you and your spouse together. In other words, do not think that you are immune from the temptation or possibility of an affair. It may start with a few simple conversations, but the enemy will look for opportunities when you are at your weakest to attack.

Look at how the writer of Proverbs painted a picture of the dangers we face:

> **Proverbs 5:15-23** Drink water from your own well—share your love only with your wife. Why spill the water of your springs in the streets, having sex with just anyone? You should reserve it for yourselves. Never share it with strangers. Let your wife be a fountain of blessing for you. Rejoice in the wife of your youth. She is a loving deer, a graceful doe. Let her breasts satisfy you always. May you always be captivated by her love. Why be captivated, my son, by an immoral woman, or fondle the breasts of a promiscuous woman? For the lord sees clearly what a man does, examining every path he takes. An evil man is held captive by his own sins; they are ropes that catch and hold him. He will die for lack of self-control; he will be lost because of his great foolishness.

> **Proverbs 7:21-23** So she seduced him with her pretty speech and enticed him with her flattery. He followed her at once, like an ox going to the slaughter. He was like a stag caught in a trap, awaiting the arrow that would pierce its heart. He was like a bird flying into a snare, little knowing it would cost him his life.

While these passages may seem to apply primarily to men, we would urge women as you read them to simply replace a few pronouns. For example,

"...Rejoice in the husband of your youth." And, "...he enticed her with his flattery..." It is not too difficult to see that the danger of infidelity is lurking and waiting to tear marriages apart. What more effective way does the enemy have to accomplish his goals to steal, kill, and destroy than to rip apart the very fabric of society that God ordained from the beginning?

Different Wiring
As we discussed in Chapter 2 on communications and roles, we believe God wired up men and women very differently. This is almost always true regarding the topic of sex. Because of this difference, there will often be tension in marriage regarding this subject. However, God provides clear guidance:

> **1 Corinthians 7:1-5** Now regarding the questions you asked in your letter. Yes, it is good to abstain from sexual relations. But because there is so much sexual immorality, each man should have his own wife, and each woman should have her own husband. The husband should fulfill his wife's sexual needs, and the wife should fulfill her husband's needs. The wife gives authority over her body to her husband, and the husband gives authority over his body to his wife. Do not deprive each other of sexual relations, unless you both agree to refrain from sexual intimacy for a limited time so you can give yourselves more completely to prayer. Afterward, you should come together again so that Satan won't be able to tempt you because of your lack of self-control.

An analogy that we've heard that helped us understand each other's differences better is this: men are like microwaves and women are like crock-pots. Generally, men are ready for sex just about anytime, anywhere. A man's emotional state has very little impact on his ability to perform. On the other hand, women being more emotionally driven, typically take much longer to prepare for intimacy. Husbands need to learn what fills their wife's emotional tank and be patient and considerate with them. Women need to understand that their mate is not abnormal if he is regularly thinking, hinting, and expressing interest in sex.

Susan's Advice to Women
Ladies, there will always be someone willing to have sex with your (future) husband! This may sound like hyperbole, but it is true. There are women out there who do not care if he has a ring on his finger. Some might even consider it a personal challenge to make a man (your husband) fall. If you want to help protect your man from temptation, you will want to satisfy his sexual needs regularly. Before you balk at that last sentence, please read on.

The passage we just read from I Corinthians chapter 7 makes it clear that we are not to deprive each other sexually. The passage further indicates that if we are not meeting each other's needs in this area, it gives the enemy a foothold to tempt us – and men, unfortunately, are much more vulnerable to this type of temptation.

So, how often is regular? That is the million dollar question! According to Focus on the Family's website, there is no such thing as "normal" in this regard since researchers don't agree on how often the average couple has sex. One study they cited indicated that the largest percentage of couples reporting in a study said they had intercourse three times a week.[4] However, they go on to state that statistics on sexual behavior can be quite misleading. Further, oversimplifying the issue with basic math can lead to anxiety and stress. Many Hollywood movies and TV shows portray couples having sex practically every day. Nothing we have read indicates that this is the norm. The important thing to remember is that our goal should be selflessness. Have very open and honest discussions about this with your spouse and decide what would be considered "regular" to both of you. Then, BE REGULAR! Husbands and wives both should work toward meeting a goal that makes both of you happy. You know the word - compromise.

Lastly, I want to be very frank with you because I fully believe in the importance of sex in marriage. First, the excuse of a headache no longer works as there are medical articles indicating that sexual intercourse actually helps with blood flow, relieving headaches. Second, there are times you may not feel like it, but I would encourage you to enjoy the journey. Also, think about this. There are times your husband will do things for you that he won't necessarily enjoy, but he knows

---

[4] *Understanding Human Sexuality* by Janet Shibley Hyde and John D. DeLamater (McGraw-Hill, 1997)

it's important to you so he does it. Third, if you continually have anxiety about sex, pray and ask God to reveal to you exactly why you are feeling this way. He is faithful and He will show you exactly what you need to do. If there are unresolved emotional issues, professional counseling may be warranted.

Buddy's Advice to Men
Men, you may have just read Susan's advice and are all excited about actually having research to cite about how regular your sex life should be. Cool your jets for a moment. I want to ask you a few questions to gage whether you have a right to complain. Is your quiet time with God consistent? Are you praying regularly with your wife? Are you taking the family to church each week? If you have kids, are you praying with them and engaged in their lives? Are you taking your wife on dates? Are you actively listening to her share her thoughts and dreams with you? Are you learning her love language and filling her emotional tank? If you answered yes to all of these questions, then my guess is you have no complaints about your sex life.

Men, your wife is longing for spiritual leadership. If you answered no to the first two questions, then you need to reprioritize. I can promise you that if you get these priorities straight, then your love life will dramatically improve.

Keep the Romance Alive
While you are dating or early-on in your marriage, romance is usually easy. However, when kids and mortgages come along, it will take a little more

intentionality to preserve that spark. As a couple, you need to learn to communicate and plan activities to fan the flames of romance.

Take a look at several scriptures and note the way these men and women communicated their love to their spouse:

> **Proverbs 31:28-30** Her children stand and bless her. Her husband praises her: "There are many virtuous and capable women in the world, but you surpass them all!" Charm is deceptive, and beauty does not last; but a woman who fears the lord will be greatly praised.

> **Song of Solomon 5:10-16** My lover is dark and dazzling, better than ten thousand others! His head is finest gold, his wavy hair is black as a raven. His eyes sparkle like doves beside springs of water; they are set like jewels washed in milk. His cheeks are like gardens of spices giving off fragrance. His lips are like lilies, perfumed with myrrh. His arms are like rounded bars of gold, set with beryl. His body is like bright ivory, glowing with lapis lazuli. His legs are like marble pillars set in sockets of finest gold. His posture is stately, like the noble cedars of Lebanon. His mouth is sweetness itself; he is desirable in every way. Such, O women of Jerusalem, is my lover, my friend.

What woman does not want to hear her husband praise her and say she surpasses all other women? What husband would not want to be called dazzling? Yes, you will likely have different terms or descriptors that you use for your spouse, but the principle is the same. We have our own unique terms of endearment that we use with each other. Whether we leave notes or text each other, we daily share our love and affection for one another, even after 27 years.

Another thing that we love to do together is take road trips. There are even examples of that in the Bible believe it or not:

> **Song of Solomon 7:10-12** I am my lover's, and he claims me as his own. Come, my love, let us go out to the fields and spend the night among the wildflowers. Let us get up early and go to the vineyards to see if the grapevines have budded, if the blossoms have opened, and if the pomegranates have bloomed. There I will give you my love.

Take time to get away together regularly. It breaks the monotony and gives you a chance to relax and focus on each other away from work, kids, and other responsibilities. Some of our most memorable times together involve weekends away sharing life and love. Sex is a beautiful, God-ordained, integral part of your marriage. Do not neglect nurturing this part of your relationship that is unlike any other earthly bond you have. Like anything else, if you want it to be "successful" (for lack of a better term), you have to make it a priority. Do not leave each other with leftovers. God wants your marriage to be successful, and God will bless your love life if you seek obedience to Him in this area.

Questions to Discuss Together

1. Have you both remained sexually pure for your spouse? If not, be honest about your past relationships.

2. What misconceptions about sex have you been taught or just picked up from the world around you (e.g. it's ok to do it with anyone you love or it's dirty and only for making babies)?

3. Have you ever been sexually abused or molested? If so, have you sought professional counseling to deal with it? Have you been able to forgive?

4. Do you have any struggles with pornography, romance novels, or anything else that creates fantasies with someone other than your spouse (fiancé)?

5. Do you have any close relationships with friends of the opposite sex? If so, discuss how you plan to guard against impropriety.

6. How do you feel about watching R-rated movies with sex scenes? How does it affect your thought life?

7. Are you more romantic or pragmatic? What fills your emotional tank?

8. How often is "regular" for you? If your answers are different, what can you each do to get closer to the same answer?

9. Do you have terms of endearment for each other? What are your favorites that your spouse (fiancé) uses for you?

10. What are your favorite activities together? Are there changes you need to make in your schedules to allow for more time alone together?

Chapter 6: Parenting

Thoughts and reactions vary in people's minds when it comes to the topic of parenting. For some, the thought of having a house full of children elicits happy feelings. For others, because of hurtful or not-so-positive childhood experiences, it's ominous to think of even having one child. While parenting is one of the most difficult responsibilities in the world, it is also one of the most rewarding.

A word to single parents. You have a tough job. We know that because we know how tough it is for two parents to raise kids. But, we hope you know that God loves you and wants the best for you and your children. We hope that you find encouragement and support not only in the pages that follow, but in a healthy church that loves you and can partner with you to raise godly children.

Here's a news flash: There are no perfect parents. We are all flawed and faulty human beings. However, if we are willing to admit that and seek help from godly friends and resources, God can overcome our imperfections.

Here's another news flash: You can gage the health of a society by the health of its families. Our society seems to be getting less healthy. Chaos permeates classrooms and young people are exposed to other dire issues such as gangs, drugs, and human trafficking. We might ask God why He doesn't intercede, and He might be answering that He can and will through parents who are intentional about raising godly children. Perhaps He will use us to help turn things around in our homes and our society.

We realize that entire books are written on the subject of parenting. We will only scratch the surface here in this chapter. However, we want to cover several important topics that you will want to discuss as a couple whether you are not yet parents or are working through parenting issues.

Intentionality and Mission

Intentionality means to be deliberate or premeditated. We have learned that we cannot just fly by the seat of our pants with this huge responsibility. Here's an analogy: what if you need some sort of certification or continuing education unit or even a degree? Perhaps your career would be enhanced with a promotion or raise. Maybe it would improve your resume for a job you are seeking. You would likely enroll in a class, study hard, or take practice tests. You might watch videos or tutorials. You might even hire a tutor if you need extra help. You would be very intentional and deliberate about earning this credit or credential. That is how we need to approach parenting. Very intentionally.

King Solomon was one of the wisest men to ever walk the face of the earth. He was very intentional about imparting wisdom to his children. Here's how he starts the book of Proverbs:

Proverbs 1:1-7 These are the proverbs of Solomon, David's son, king of Israel. Their purpose is to teach people wisdom and discipline, to help them understand the insights of the wise. Their purpose is to teach people to live disciplined and successful lives, to help them do what is right, just, and fair. These proverbs will give insight to the simple, knowledge and discernment to the young. Let the wise listen to these proverbs and become even wiser. Let those with understanding receive guidance by exploring the meaning in these proverbs and parables, the words of the wise and their riddles. Fear of the lord is the foundation of true knowledge, but fools despise wisdom and discipline.

He begins verse eight, and each subsequent chapter through chapter 7, with the phrase "my child," "my son," or "my children." He very deliberately and intentionally imparts what he knows to be godly principles to his offspring. God knowing how valuable that would be for us, preserved those nuggets of sagacity for us through the centuries. We encourage you to read through Proverbs chapters one through seven to gain a sense of the priority and mission God has for us as parents.

We see God's intentionality and mission for children clearly in His description of His own son as he was growing up.

> **Luke 2:52** Jesus grew in wisdom and in stature and in favor with God and all the people.

Notice it says that Jesus grew intellectually, physically, spiritually, and socially. So it would seem logical that we need to make sure our kids go to school and do their homework, we need to make sure they eat right and get exercise, and we need to make sure our kids learn to interact with others in a healthy way. But, our most important role is that of nurturing our child's spirit. Turning again to Proverbs:

> **Proverbs 22:6** Train up a child in the way he should go, and when he is old he will not depart from it. (WEB)

This verse gives the sense of spiritual training and discipline. The phrase "in the way he should go" could be translated "the way she is bent." Think of a branch of a tree and how it grows and twists and turns. There is a sense of learning how God wired up your son or daughter and discovering how your children are gifted and how they learn. Are they left brained or right brained? Are they leaders or followers? As you become a student of your child, you learn about their spiritual gifts so you can help them use those gifts for the Kingdom.

The book of Ephesians gives some insight into the purpose of spiritual gifts:

Ephesians 4:11-13 Now these are the gifts Christ gave to the church: the apostles, the prophets, the evangelists, and the pastors and teachers. Their responsibility is to equip God's people to do his work and build up the church, the body of Christ. This will continue until we all come to such unity in our faith and knowledge of God's Son that we will be mature in the Lord, measuring up to the full and complete standard of Christ.

Note that spiritual gifts are not just imparted to adults. The scriptures say that all who are in Christ are given spiritual gifts to serve. An important job as a parent is to help your child understand their giftedness and put those gifts into practice.

As parents, we also have to be diligent and intentional about our kids' friends. This is a really critical issue as described in the New Testament:

I Corinthians 15:33 Do not be misled: "Bad company corrupts good character." (NIV)

Our Pastor, Greg Wigfield, taught on at least one occasion about dialing up and dialing down certain relationships. When our boys were younger, we took that to heart and we encouraged certain relationships and learned to say yes as often as we could about sleepovers and other activities. If our sons were friends with boys that we did not know or if we did not know their parents, we would have sleepovers at our house, typically on Saturday night, so their friends could go to church with us the next day. Then, when we had to say no, we had stored up enough "yeses" so that the inevitable "you never let us do anything" statement was easily dismissed.

As parents, we are primarily responsible to teach our own kids to love and fear and serve God. This has been a principle handed down through the generations from the days of Moses:

> **Deuteronomy 6:6-7** And you must commit yourselves wholeheartedly to these commands that I am giving you today. Repeat them again and again to your children. Talk about them when you are at home and when you are on the road, when you are going to bed and when you are getting up.

Pastors and youth group leaders will supplement and reinforce these principles, but a pastor's job is to help equip parents for this role – it is not to replace a parent in this role. You might think about going out of the country on a mission trip and even taking your children when they are old enough. That is a good thing and we would encourage that. But, your children are your primary mission field, and that is a lifelong mission. It is not Mission Impossible, so your mission – should you choose to accept it, is to take-on your God-given responsibility to instruct your children in His ways.

We are not downplaying the importance of church in your children's lives. One very deliberate and intentional way to instruct your children in God's ways is to be actively committed and involved in the local church as the writer of Hebrews encourages:

> **Hebrews 10:25** And let us not neglect our meeting together, as some people do, but encourage one another, especially now that the day of his return is drawing near.

Woody Allen is quoted as saying that 80% of success in life is showing up. Part of learning to love God is by serving him. Using our time, talent, and treasure to serve the Kingdom. It is vitally important that we set the pace as parents and show up on Sunday to worship our Creator and also when there are opportunities in the local church to serve. There will be many distractions along the way. Sports, music, and school activities are examples of good things that can impede involvement in great things. Please do not let "activities" trump ministry.

Also, don't fall for the false argument that if you force them to go they will become resentful. You don't buy that argument when it comes to them going to school or brushing their teeth do you? We would argue that their spiritual development is even more important than school and should be prioritized accordingly.

Avoid Favoritism
Don't play favorites with your children – God doesn't. God loves unconditionally as seen in the following verse:

Romans 3:22 We are made right with God by placing our faith in Jesus Christ. And this is true for everyone who believes, no matter who we are.

In the Old Testament story about Jacob and his twelve sons, Jacob favored his son Joseph over his other sons. Here is a synopsis from Genesis:

Genesis 37:3-4 Jacob loved Joseph more than any of his other children because Joseph had been born to him in his old age. So one day Jacob had a special gift made for Joseph—a beautiful robe. But his brothers hated Joseph because their father loved him more than the rest of them. They couldn't say a kind word to him.

Look at the pain and suffering Jacob caused Joseph because of favoritism. Joseph's brothers hated him so much they sold him as a slave when he was only a teenager. Because of other various circumstances, he spent years in prison. Yes, God redeemed his life and used Joseph for His glory, but the consequences of Jacob's actions were horrible. You may butt heads with one of your kids, but one of you has to be the adult. You do not want to do damage that could have long-term consequences in your relationship with one or more of your children. It is important to love all of your children unconditionally and treat them equally.

Priorities

Prioritize your children. Jesus did. Here is how He responded to children:

> **Matthew 19:13-15** One day some parents brought their children to Jesus so he could lay his hands on them and pray for them. But the disciples scolded the parents for bothering him. But Jesus said, "Let the children come to me. Don't stop them! For the Kingdom of Heaven belongs to those who are like these children." And he placed his hands on their heads and blessed them before he left.

Your children are not an inconvenience. God gave them to you to raise. In fact, here's what Solomon recorded for us:

> **Psalm 127:3** Children are a gift from the LORD; they are a reward from him.

In terms of priority, your children should be number three behind Jesus and your spouse. There's a song called "Cats in the Cradle" by Harry Chapin that illustrates the potential consequence of neglecting this important relationship. It starts out describing a father too busy to be an integral part of his son's life while he was growing up. Despite his father's absence, the boy declared he was going to grow up to be just like his dad. Several verses then describe him growing up and heading off to college. The final verse portrays their relationship later in life when the father asks to spend time with his son. His son's response was that he just couldn't find the time. The father's final words capture the essence of the song, "...it occurred to me, he'd grown up just like me."

We have heard it said that when it comes to your kids, more is caught than taught. Our kids get it – they know what our priorities are. When we were first married, we heard a speaker say once, that one of the best things dads can do to provide stability and security for their kids is to make sure they understand that you love Jesus and you love their mother.

One way to prioritize them is to attempt, if possible, to have one parent be at home full time with your children when they are growing up. We were blessed in that regard, but it happened in part, based on decisions we made early-on about our lifestyle. Knowing that we wanted to have Susan be at home with our boys after they were born, we lived in a way that allowed us to get by on Buddy's salary alone. Even though Susan had two business degrees and was very successful in the corporate world prior to kids, we planned ahead and didn't let the bank or realtors convince us to purchase a house that would require two incomes to make ends meet. Susan fully enjoyed staying home with her babies and has no regrets. Looking back, we acknowledge that we would not trade it for anything. Any. Thing!

Discipline
There are many books and resources available regarding the subject of discipline. As we sought godly counsel and studied those resources ourselves, we

quickly realized that God's Word has plenty to say about the subject. So we aligned our discipline methods with the Bible and with resources from organizations that shared that same philosophy. It all starts by figuring out who is going to be in charge:

> **Ephesians 6:1** Children, obey your parents because you belong to the Lord, for this is the right thing to do.

This may seem like a fairly obvious point, but either because of pop psychology or just some parents' misguided perception that they have to be friends with their kids, the principle of obedience to parents is often lacking in some families. What we then see in society is that lack of obedience in the home often translates to lack of respect for authority at school, in the workplace, and even with law enforcement.

At the other extreme is parenting that is too harsh or even abusive. That's why this passage goes on a few verses later with instructions to fathers:

> **Ephesians 6:4** Fathers, do not provoke your children to anger by the way you treat them. Rather, bring them up with the discipline and instruction that comes from the Lord.

The opposite of provoking children to anger is encouragement. Note that there is a difference between praise and encouragement. Praise is based on some type of accomplishment or achievement.

Encouragement is unconditional – based on love and relationship.

So God says there is a balance. Children are to learn to obey their parents. Parents are to impart discipline in a way that is not harsh, but rather encouraging. With that balance in mind, let's look to the Old Testament for some practical guidance:

> **Proverbs 13:24** Those who spare the rod of discipline hate their children. Those who love their children care enough to discipline them.

> **Proverbs 22:15** A youngster's heart is filled with foolishness, but physical discipline will drive it far away.

> **Proverbs 23:13-15** Don't fail to discipline your children. The rod of punishment won't kill them. Physical discipline may well save them from death. My child, if your heart is wise, my own heart will rejoice!

Notice in each of these verses the connection of love with discipline. Here's a rhetorical question: do you love your children? Some of you may say it depends on what day you ask. Of course, we all love our children and want the best for them. God says, if you love them you care enough to discipline them. That's why he disciplines us because he loves us:

Hebrews 12:6 "For the lord disciplines those he loves, and he punishes each one he accepts as his child."

This then leads to the topic of spanking. Corporal punishment is a controversial topic. You may have very strong opinions about this subject based on your childhood or other factors. First, let us be very clear that we are opposed to any form of child abuse – either verbal or physical. However, we can speak with confidence on this subject knowing what God's Word says. One morning as we were riding to church together, we heard a local pastor in one of the larger churches in our area speaking about this subject on the radio. He said "I didn't write this in the Bible – God did – so we need to do what it says!" So, please hear us out – give us a chance to share a few points.

We believe there is an appropriate place for firm, loving discipline with our children. When we first had children, we had only our own experience as children from which to draw, but we both felt it was very important to do things God's way. So we became students of Dr. James Dobson, and a ministry he started called Focus on the Family. He authored a book called Dare to Discipline, which is still available today and a great resource. We would encourage you to get it and use it to go beyond the brief discussion we will have here. Many of the following principles are gleaned from the Focus on the Family website.

First, let's discuss the difference between willful, defiant disobedience versus childish irresponsibility.

Willful, defiant disobedience is when your child looks you in the eye and does exactly the opposite of what you just told them not to do. If you say come here and they run the other way or if you say don't throw that and they throw it, these are examples of misbehavior that require swift and firm but loving discipline.

Contrast the behavior just described to examples such as leaving the bike out in the rain, forgetting their lunch or backpack for school, or forgetting to feed the dog. These are examples of childish irresponsibility that deserve consequences, but perhaps not quite at the same level of intensity.

We believe firm, loving discipline involving spanking is to deal with willful defiance. It involves immediate, firm, and consistent consequences. We do not believe that spankings are appropriate for children 18 months old or younger. However, for children ages 1½ to 3½ years of age, reasoning and taking away privileges simply is not effective, and spanking is likely most effective for this age range. For children three to five years of age, spanking, time-outs, and other consequences such as taking away privileges can be used together as part of a diverse discipline plan. Solely relying on one method will become less effective as a child matures. For many school-aged children, removal of privileges is actually more "painful" than a spanking. In no instance should spanking be administered harshly or impulsively. Spanking an adolescent or teenager is almost always a serious mistake.

A proper technique involves escorting or sending the child to a designated room. Spanking should never be done publicly or in front of others, including siblings. You should review the offense beforehand so that they understand the reason for the discipline. A spank is intended to sting not bruise and should simply involve a few "swats" to the fatty part of the buttocks. After the punishment, put them in your lap and hug them and express your love for your child. Explain that it is because you love them that you want them to learn right from wrong and obedience to God.

Whatever form of discipline you choose, you and your spouse need to decide together. Seek godly counsel from people you know and trust and who display evidence of obedient children. More important than any of this is to pray fervently for wisdom and courage to discipline.

Life Lessons
Let us share an example of our sons displaying childish irresponsibility and turning that into a life lesson. When John and Joshua were around ten and eight years old, respectively, Buddy took them to a grocery store to pick up a few items. It was an older store with a bathroom in an employee area, which Buddy had to use. He instructed the boys to wait together in the coffee aisle, just outside the door to the employee area, knowing he would be back momentarily - in hindsight, probably a lapse in judgment. He returned to find the boys standing together looking sheepishly at their feet with a store employee nearby. Accusingly, she asked "Are these

your boys?" Buddy responded affirmatively and asked if there was a problem. "Are you planning to purchase all the coffee beans your boys just dispensed into these bags and all over the floor?" she queried. Buddy answered that he would of course take care of it. "Never mind," she countered, "just move along and I'll get this mess cleaned up." Without purchasing whatever groceries they came for, Buddy and the boys headed for the car and home.

Buddy was fuming all the way home trying to figure out an appropriate punishment. After talking it over with Susan, we decided that the boys would dig into their piggy banks for the amount to cover the coffee beans. Buddy took them back to the store to speak with the manager. God provided a saintly, gray-haired, grandfatherly gentleman to deal with the situation. Nervously the boys explained the situation to him and offered to pay for the damage. He pondered for a moment and told John and Joshua that he was proud of them for doing the right thing and telling the truth. He said that instead of paying him, he would like for them to give the money to their favorite charity or church. We all left the store relieved that God had provided such a wise, gentle person to teach a valuable life lesson. John and Josh fulfilled their promise and placed the money in the church offering the following Sunday. More importantly, they learned that there are consequences to bad behavior – sometimes more painful than a spanking!

We tell that story to illustrate that there is no cookbook approach to discipline. The principle is that we discipline our children because we love them and that's what God asks us to do as their caretakers for the brief time they are in our care.

A final word on discipline involves choosing your battles. This is especially important for teenagers. One word of advice we received was this: if it can grow back, grow in, be cut off, or washed off, you might want to let it go. Purple hair will eventually grow out and can be cut off. A tattoo is a little different story. Decide if it's a hill you want to die on. We would often discuss these concepts together when trying to decide how to handle a situation. A messy room might drive you crazy, but you can always shut the door. If they are going to church, hanging out with good friends, and making good grades perhaps a messy room is something you can live with.

Chores and Money
Other important and related principles to teach our kids involve chores and handling money. Much of what we discussed in the chapter on Money is appropriate to teach children as they become mature enough to grasp the concepts. Again, there are many different approaches to this, so what we share are a few ideas and methods that worked reasonably well for us.

The first principle is learning a work ethic. From a very young age, we think it is important that children learn to contribute to the structure and function of a home by doing age appropriate chores. Whether that involves putting away toys, helping with dishes and laundry, or even pulling weeds in the flower bed or garden, learning that there is an expectation that everyone contributes to the function of the home is vital. This not only teaches self-discipline that can help with other issues like school work, but teaches a work ethic that will benefit them for life.

The Bible is clear that God wired us up to labor and be productive. Both the Old and New Testaments give us insight in that regard:

> **Ecclesiastes 5:18-19** Even so, I have noticed one thing, at least, that is good. It is good for people to eat, drink, and enjoy their work under the sun during the short life God has given them, and to accept their lot in life. And it is a good thing to receive wealth from God and the good health to enjoy it. To enjoy your work and accept your lot in life—this is indeed a gift from God.

> **2 Thessalonians 3:6-12** And now, dear brothers and sisters, we give you this command in the name of our Lord Jesus Christ: Stay away from all believers who live idle lives and don't follow the tradition they received from us. For you know that you ought to imitate us. We were not idle when we were with you. We never accepted food from anyone without paying for it. We worked hard day and night so we would not be a burden to any of you. We certainly had the right to ask you to feed us, but we wanted to give you an example to follow. Even while we were with you, we

gave you this command: "Those unwilling to work will not get to eat." Yet we hear that some of you are living idle lives, refusing to work and meddling in other people's business. We command such people and urge them in the name of the Lord Jesus Christ to settle down and work to earn their own living.

Proverbs 6:6-8 Go to the ant, you sluggard; consider its ways and be wise! It has no commander, no overseer or ruler, yet it stores its provisions in summer and gathers its food at harvest. (NIV)

We don't want to raise a bunch of sluggards do we? Of course not, and training them to do chores is a great way to avoid that. From a practical standpoint, chore charts are one way we used to organize and distribute responsibilities. Again, there are many resources on the internet that may work better for you and your family. The key is being intentional and consistent. Teaching our children the value of work is a godly principle.

Another principle is teaching children how to handle money. We teach the concepts of chores and money together, because they are often related. Some people believe that tying an allowance to chores is a good way to teach the concept of working later in life for a paycheck. Others believe that there are certain "chores" that are required without pay just to keep the household functioning and then there are "special projects" that a child can do to earn money. An example is washing the car. If you would normally pay a certain amount to have your car washed and your child is willing to do that job, they could be paid for that. We actually employed both methods. We set a certain benchmark allowance and if all the chores for the week were checked off the list, they received the full amount. If all the chores were not completed or not done to a certain standard, there were deductions. We also gave opportunities for them to earn money above their allowance with special projects.

By the time our boys were 14 and our state laws allowed them to get a part-time job, they were bagging groceries and working at the outlet mall weekends and summers. They then truly learned what it meant to "punch the clock" and have a boss to answer to besides mom and dad.

Another idea we learned from friends involved getting them a checking account to manage their money. At age 13, Susan took them to our bank to get them signed up for a checking account tied to our accounts. In addition to the money they were earning with their part-time jobs, we transitioned them away from their allowance to a lump sum amount for the year (that didn't eliminate the chores they were still required to do at home by the way). The lump sum consisted of the amount we would normally spend on them in a year for clothing, school supplies, gifts they would give friends for birthdays, etc. The first year we did that with John (around 10 years ago), we calculated $800 for the year. That of course will vary for you today depending on your location and inflation. But they were free to manage that money for the year. If they decided to blow it all on a dirt bike, they would wear the same clothes all year. If they managed it well and had money left over by their next birthday, they could keep the balance. It allowed them the freedom to shop for their own clothes without mom and dad breathing down their neck and taught them to be responsible and accountable for their finances. Of course, they did not have carte blanche to do whatever they wanted with the money. There should always be a common sense parental override at the ready if teenagers are about to do something illegal or inappropriate. If they are about to get a tattoo or start day trading with the money, you will definitely want to weigh in.

As we outlined in the Money chapter, tithing is the most important principle for any Christian, and it is the first thing you'll want to teach your kids when it comes to handling money. Teach them as soon as you start an allowance or whenever they begin to receive money that the first fruits belong to God. We talked about the 10-10-80 rule for you as a couple. You might want to employ that with your kids, but with twist: the first ten percent to God, 10 percent to spend, and 80 percent for savings.

Blessing Your Children
Blessing your children is a powerful biblical concept. In Old Testament times, there was often a prophetic meaning to the spoken blessing. Let's look at an example of Isaac, Esau, and Jacob:

Genesis 27:2-4 Isaac said, "I am now an old man and don't know the day of my death. Now then, get your equipment—your quiver and bow—and go out to the open country to hunt some wild game for me. Prepare me the kind of tasty food I like and bring it to me to eat, so that I may give you my blessing before I die."

This is literally such a big deal that Esau's brother Jacob and Jacob's mother conspired to steal the blessing from Esau. It is still a big deal today and we would encourage you to find ways to provide a spiritual blessing on your children as they grow up. Use events like birthdays, graduations, or weddings to publicly declare those blessings.

When John and Joshua were 13 and 11, respectively, Buddy partnered with three other dads at Destiny Church in Leesburg, Virginia who had boys about the same age as John and Joshua. Together, the four dads read a book called "Raising a Modern Day Knight" by Robert Lewis. Over the years, they planned ceremonies and celebrations to mark certain significant events in the lives of their sons including birthdays, transitioning to high school, graduating from high school, and marriage. The ceremonies in particular included times to publicly pronounce a blessing on the boys as they reached a milestone in their lives. These were often very emotional, particularly for the dads.

The ceremony associated with marriage includes what is called "The Oath." When our oldest son John married Blake in 2015, Buddy had the opportunity to share a very personal blessing at the rehearsal dinner the night before the wedding. Here is a portion of what he shared:

> John, I am so proud of the godly man you have become. You are making responsible decisions and using the gifts God has given you and you are seeing blessings in your life because of it. The woman standing next to you and the vows you will make to her tomorrow represent the second most important decision of your life in my opinion. With God's leading, you have chosen well and I am so very proud of you and I love you.
>
> Blake, tomorrow is the culmination of 22 years of prayer and discipline and tears and laughter that have shaped the man standing next to you. Ten of those years have also been shaped by this group standing here. We pray that we have helped prepare him to love you, protect you, and provide spiritual leadership in your marriage.

We said earlier that parenting is one of the most challenging, but also one of the most rewarding jobs God has given us. What a reward to be able to stand with our son and future daughter-in-law and speak those words of blessing.

We are not Alone

While we need to be intentional about raising our children, we do not have to tackle it alone. We began this chapter saying there are no perfect parents. We're going to qualify that statement: there is one perfect parent! God loves us and he loves our kids – even more than we do. He is our standard – He is our role model. His Word gives us guidance, but most importantly, He has given us who are followers of Jesus, the Holy Spirit. We have power – the same power that raised Jesus from the dead. That power can help us to have the wisdom, courage, and intentionality we need to raise kids God's way.

War or Peace: Issues That Impact Marriage

Questions to Discuss Together

1. How many children would you like to have?

2. Will you attempt to have one parent be at home with the children when they are growing up?

3. What are some things you will teach your children that are different from what your parents taught you? What things will you teach that are the same?

4. What if kids' activities conflict with church? What takes priority?

5. Will you have your children do chores? Should children get paid for chores?

6. Do you think it is good for a teenager to manage a lump-sum of their annual expenses? What if they want to spend a large portion of it on something frivolous?

7. Do you think spanking is an appropriate form of discipline? If not, how will you discipline?

8. Did your parents play favorites with you or your siblings? Do you find yourself tempted to play favorites with your children?

9. How will you guide your children in their selection of friends?

10. What are some ways you can express blessing over your children?

Resources

Dr. James Dobson's Family Talk -
www.drjamesdobson.org

Family Life - www.familylife.com

Focus on the Family - www.focusonthefamily.com

Love and Respect - www.loveandrespect.com

Love Dare - www.thelovedarebook.com

Marriage Builders - www.marriagebuilders.com

Marriage by the Book - www.marriagebythebook.org

Marriage Matters - www.marriagematters.ws

Marriage Missions - www.marriagemissions.com

Marriage Today - www.marriagetoday.com

Raising a Modern Day Knight - www.rmdk.com

Start Marriage Right - www.startmarriageright.com

War or Peace: Issues That Impact Marriage -
www.warorpeace.family

About the Authors

Susan grew up in Seattle and loves the Pacific Northwest. She enjoys cooking from scratch, sewing, and home decorating. She has dual undergraduate business degrees in marketing and management and a master's degree in education. She has been an accountant, business manager, and school teacher, but Buddy thinks her most important job was as a stay-at-home mom when their sons were young.

Buddy grew up on a farm in Virginia and is a weekend warrior and DIYer. He has an engineering bachelor's degree and is a professional engineer and die-hard Virginia Tech fan. He is an associate pastor at Destiny Church in Leesburg, Virginia where he and his family have served for over 15 years.

Buddy and Susan have two grown sons, John and Joshua. John's wife Blake is the newest addition to their family.

While not professional counselors, the Showalters enjoy sharing their 27-plus years of marital and parenting experience with couples contemplating marriage or dealing with family issues.

Made in the USA
Lexington, KY
12 January 2017